The halogen oven cookbook

Maryanne Madden

hamlyn

An Hachette UK Company
www.hachette.co.uk

First published in Great Britain in 2010 by
Hamlyn, a division of Octopus Publishing
Group Ltd
Endeavour House
189 Shaftesbury Avenue
London
WC2H 8JY
www.octopusbooksusa.com

Distributed in the U.S. and Canada by
Octopus Books USA:
c/o Hachette Book Group
237 Park Avenue
New York, NY 10017

Maryanne Madden asserts the moral right to
be identified as the author of this work.

ISBN 978-0-600-62181-2

Printed and bound in the UK

10 9 8 7 6 5 4 3 2 1

Read your halogen oven manual before
you begin and preheat the halogen oven if
required according to the manufacturer's
instructions. Because halogen ovens vary
slightly from manufacturer to manufacturer,
check recipe timings with the manufacturer's
directions for a recipe using the same
ingredients. All recipes for this book were
tested in a Pro Cooks Halogen Oven.

Standard level spoon measures are used in
all recipes:
1 tablespoon = one 15 ml spoon
1 teaspoon = one 5 ml spoon

Medium eggs have been used throughout.

Fresh herbs should be used unless
otherwise stated.

A few recipes contain nuts and nut
derivatives. Anyone with a known nut
allergy must avoid these.

This book contains some dishes made with
raw or lightly cooked eggs. It is prudent for
more vulnerable people such as pregnant
and nursing mothers, invalids, the elderly,
babies and young children to avoid raw or
lightly cooked eggs.

contents

introduction

Halogen ovens use innovative halogen technology to cook almost any type of food. These compact table-top ovens are convenient and easy to use, and they are generally much quicker than a conventional oven. The tiered racks make it possible to cook food quickly and allow fat to drain away, making the food prepared by this relatively new way of cooking both tasty and healthy.

This cookbook contains over 100 recipes to cook in your halogen oven. The dishes range from basic roast meat recipes to help you get started with your oven to more complicated fish and vegetable dishes and desserts and bakes. The instructions are easy to follow and provide you with a wide variety of ways to use your halogen oven, whether you are cooking for the whole family or making a quick lunch to eat alone or enjoy with friends.

all about halogen ovens

Halogen ovens work by means of an infrared halogen element that is sited in the lid. This heats up almost instantly, so you will find that your halogen oven is more cost-efficient than a conventional stove because you do not have to preheat it. In addition, most cooking times are about 40 percent less than in an ordinary oven, again saving money. Moreover, the fan-assisted air circulation cooks food evenly, meaning that it is usually unnecessary to turn items.

You can use your halogen oven to bake, roast, steam, and broil food, and some models also have a thaw function, allowing you to cook frozen foods without waiting for them to defrost.

Unlike a microwave oven, a halogen oven will brown food just like a conventional oven, making it easy to prepare succulent roast meats, such as chicken and pork, with crisp, crunchy skin and crackling.

The arrangement of racks within the halogen oven means that there is ample room to cook a whole meal for your family, including plenty of vegetables, or a simple small meal for one person, and once you have got used to using your oven you will find that it is versatile, economical, and much easier to clean than a conventional oven.

halogen oven basics

Most ovens are supplied with:

- Base stand and housing
- Glass bowl
- Removable glass lid with halogen element and electrical lead
- Steel racks
- Steel handles so that you can safely move the racks and other containers.

The glass bowl is usually around 12–13 inches wide and about 7 inches deep.

When you are using your halogen oven it's important that you make full use of all accessories that are supplied. Most models are equipped with two cooking racks—an upper and a lower one—which can be used alone or in combination to increase the number of dishes you can cook at the same time. Because the racks raise the food from the base of the oven, the food will be cooked more quickly than if it is sitting directly in the base of the bowl. Although you won't damage the bowl by placing food in it, it will take longer to cook.

self-cleaning function

The glass bowl can be easily washed in hot soapy water or in your dishwasher, but if you are buying a new halogen oven it's worth looking for one with a self-cleaning function, which you can use as follows:

- Half-fill the glass bowl with hot water
- Push down the handle to lock it
- Turn the setting to the wash function
- Set the timer to the required time (usually 10–15 minutes).

Never immerse the lid in water. After use, keep it clean by wiping it with a damp cloth.

other equipment

You can use all the utensils, baking sheets, and casserole dishes that you would use in your conventional oven in your halogen oven, and, unlike in your microwave oven, you can safely use metal dishes and baking pans.

casserole dish

For most of the recipes in this book you will need a casserole dish holding about 6 cups. You will sometimes need a smaller dish and, occasionally, a larger one, so always check before you begin that your casserole dish will fit inside the glass bowl and that you can easily lift it out and into the bowl. A casserole dish that is about 9 inches across will be ideal.

Although it's possible to cook food directly in the bowl, cooking in a casserole dish that you can place on the lower rack allows the hot air to circulate around the food, cooking it more quickly and more evenly.

baking sheets

Some manufacturers supply baking sheets and roasting pans specifically for use in their halogen ovens. Round ones are especially useful and are available on the Internet. However, if you cannot find an appropriately sized baking sheet you can always cover one of the racks with kitchen foil.

kitchen foil

Many of the recipes in this book recommend that you use foil to protect food from burning or overbrowning on top. This is because the halogen oven operates in a similar way to a broiler—it will cook food on the outside more quickly than the inside—so you should cover food with foil to make sure the top doesn't burn.

If your casserole dish has a snugly fitting lid you can use the lid to cover a dish, but often the lid makes a casserole dish heavy and awkward to lift, especially when you are wearing oven mitts, while foil is light and easy to use.

getting started

To set up your halogen oven place the metal housing on a secure, perfectly flat kitchen worktop or table with easy and safe access to an electric socket. Set the glass bowl in the base. Place the lid on the bowl and push down the handle to lock it.

Plug the lead into a nearby socket and turn the timer clockwise to select the required time. At this point the power button will be on. Turn the temperature dial clockwise to the setting you want, and a light will come on. When the oven has reached the desired temperature the light will go off. It will come back on again if the temperature falls during the cooking process to indicate that the oven is heating up again. When the food is ready, which is usually indicated by a bell,

use the steel handles to take the container or racks out of the glass bowl.

The lid will be extremely hot. Do not put it directly on your kitchen worktop; instead place it on a thick cork or wooden mat.

cooking temperatures

Most halogen ovens have a lowest temperature setting of about 250°F (125°C) and a highest setting of 480°F (250°C).

You have probably noticed how similar these settings are to those of a conventional oven. However, the distinctive design of the halogen oven means that cooking times at the same temperature are greatly reduced.

which food?

You can cook almost any food in your halogen oven, and the recipes in this book include:
• Meat, poultry, and fish
• Vegetables

- Pizzas and pasta
- Bread, cakes, and pastry.

Don't forget that you might also have a thaw function on your halogen oven, which will enable you to cook frozen foods straight from the freezer. Even though frozen food will take longer to cook, it will still cook more quickly than in your conventional oven.

In general, vegetables will take longer to cook than meat, so you will often need to start cooking them first, particularly root vegetables. You can cook vegetables directly on the racks or in a casserole dish with a little water or oil.

take care

The oven's glass lid gets extremely hot, so always wear oven mitts to handle it and do not put it directly on your worktop.

- Always check that meat is completely cooked, because halogen ovens tend to brown meat quite quickly on the outside before cooking it through
- Use foil to avoid burning and overbrowning food, removing it for the last 5 minutes of the cooking time
- Keep your halogen oven clean, washing the bowl or using the self-clean function after each use and wiping the lid with a soft, damp cloth.

chicken

pot roast chicken

1 whole chicken, about 5½ lb

¼ cup butter

4 celery sticks, halved

4 carrots

4 leeks, trimmed and washed

1 garlic clove, crushed

1 bay leaf

2 tablespoons chopped parsley

Roasted Potatoes (see page 124), to serve

Put the whole chicken in a roasting pan, cover with butter, and cook in the halogen oven at 400°F (200°C) for 15–20 minutes or until the skin is golden-brown.

Remove the chicken from the oven and transfer it, together with any juices, to a deep casserole dish.

Arrange the vegetables, garlic, and herbs around the chicken. Add the giblets and pour water into the casserole, taking care that it does not quite cover the chicken.

Transfer the casserole dish to the lower rack in the halogen oven, still at 400°F (200°C), and bring to boiling point. Simmer gently for about 45 minutes (you may need to turn down the temperature).

Remove the chicken from the oven and discard the giblets. Serve with the vegetables and roasted potatoes and offer the cooking juices as a gravy.

lemon chicken

4 chicken breasts, each 3½-4 oz

2 garlic cloves, finely chopped

½ teaspoon crushed red pepper

4 lemons

To serve

couscous

Mediterranean Vegetables (see page 128)

Put the chicken breasts in a casserole dish.

Mix together the garlic and crushed pepper and sprinkle over the chicken. Squeeze the juice from the lemons, retaining the lemon halves, and pour the juice over the chicken. Allow to marinate for at least 1 hour at room temperature.

Place the lemon halves over the top of the chicken. Put the casserole on the lower rack of the halogen oven and cook at 400°F (200°C) for 25-30 minutes.

Serve with couscous and Mediterranean vegetables.

simple chicken curry

4 tablespoons malt vinegar

2 teaspoons curry powder

1 teaspoon ground cumin

1 teaspoon ground coriander

¼ teaspoon ground turmeric

1 garlic clove, crushed

½ inch fresh ginger root, peeled and crushed

4 tablespoons Demerara sugar

8 boneless, skinless chicken breasts, each 3½–4 oz, cubed

4 tablespoons olive oil

2 large onions, sliced

¼ teaspoon peppercorns

1 cup ready-to-eat dried apricots, chopped

To serve

basmati rice

naan bread

In a large bowl mix together the vinegar, curry powder, cumin, coriander, turmeric, garlic, ginger, and sugar.

Add the chicken pieces to this mixture and allow to marinate for 20 minutes or, for a really strong flavor, overnight.

Heat the oil in a large skillet and cook the onions over a medium heat for about 10 minutes or until they begin to turn golden. Add the peppercorns and cook for 20–30 seconds more.

Transfer the onions to a casserole dish and add the chicken together with any remaining marinade.

Put the casserole dish on the lower rack of the halogen oven and cook at 400°F (200°C) for about 20 minutes. Check that the chicken is cooked thoroughly and then add the apricots, cover the dish and cook for another 5 minutes.

Serve with basmati rice and naan bread.

Serves 4   Preparation time **15 minutes**   Cooking time **50–55 minutes**

caribbean chicken

1 tablespoon vegetable oil

8 chicken thighs, skin on

1 large onion, chopped

3 large garlic cloves, crushed

¾ inch fresh ginger root, peeled and grated

1 teaspoon ground cinnamon

2 teaspoons cayenne pepper

1 tablespoon all-purpose flour

1¼ cups hot chicken stock

1½ lb sweet potatoes, peeled and cubed

1¾ cups coconut milk

salt and pepper

boiled rice, to serve

Heat the oil in a skillet, add the chicken thighs, and brown all over. Remove the chicken with a slotted spoon and set aside. Drain all but 1 tablespoon of the oil from the pan.

Add the onion to the pan and cook over a medium heat until soft, stirring occasionally. Add the garlic, ginger, cinnamon and cayenne pepper and cook for 1 minute. Sprinkle with the flour, stir to combine, and cook for another minute.

Transfer the spice mixture to a casserole dish and stir in the stock. Add the sweet potato and chicken.

Put the casserole dish on the lower rack of the halogen oven and cook at 350°F (180°C) for 40 minutes.

Remove the dish from the halogen oven and let cool for a couple of minutes. Stir in the coconut milk and season to taste with salt and pepper. Serve immediately with plain boiled rice.

pesto chicken

4 boneless, skinless chicken breasts, each 3½-4 oz

4 teaspoons ready-made green pesto

¾ cup grated Parmesan cheese

12 basil leaves

3 tablespoons olive oil

1 lb baby carrots, halved

2 bell peppers, seeded and cut into chunks

1 large red onion, cut into thin wedges

salt and pepper

To serve

arugula salad

vine-ripened tomatoes

Use a sharp knife to cut a pocket in each chicken breast by slicing down one of the long sides but not cutting right through. Open up the chicken.

Spread 1 teaspoon of pesto into each pocket, adding a quarter of the Parmesan to each. Add the basil leaves, then close the pockets and secure them with toothpicks.

Transfer the chicken to a casserole dish and sprinkle with 2 tablespoons oil.

Add the vegetables to the casserole dish, tossing them in the oil to coat. Bring the chicken breasts to the top and season to taste with salt and pepper.

Sprinkle the remaining oil over the chicken and transfer to the lower rack of the halogen oven. Cook at 400°F (200°C) for 20-25 minutes or until the chicken is cooked and the vegetables are tender.

Serve the chicken with a peppery arugula salad and vine-ripened tomatoes.

Serves 4   Preparation time **15 minutes**   Cooking time **25 minutes**

chicken stroganoff

1 tablespoon butter

2 teaspoons olive oil

1 small onion, finely sliced

2 cups sliced mushrooms

5 tablespoons white wine

4 boneless, skinless chicken breasts, each 3½-4 oz, cut into strips

5 tablespoons chicken stock

1 teaspoon wholegrain mustard

⅔ cup sour cream

bunch of parsley or thyme, chopped

salt and pepper

To serve

new potatoes

baby carrots

Heat the butter and oil in a large skillet, add the onion and cook for 3-4 minutes over a medium heat until soft and beginning to brown.

Add the mushrooms to the pan and cook until soft and most of the liquid has evaporated. Add the wine, bring to a boil, and cook for 5 minutes to reduce by half.

Transfer the vegetables to a casserole dish and add the chicken. Place the casserole dish on the lower rack of the halogen oven and cook at 400°F (200°C) for 10 minutes or until the chicken is golden-brown.

Add the stock, mustard, and sour cream and cook for an additional 5 minutes or until mixture begins to boil.

Remove the top from the halogen oven and let the chicken rest for a couple of minutes. Season to taste with salt and pepper, sprinkle with the parsley or thyme, and serve with new potatoes and baby carrots.

paprika chicken

2 red onions, cut into wedges

6 garlic cloves, unpeeled

2 teaspoons paprika

1½ tablespoons olive oil

3½ lb fresh chicken

few sprigs of rosemary

2 red bell peppers, cored, seeded, and cut into wide strips

2 yellow or orange bell peppers, cored, seeded, and cut into wide strips

10 oz chorizo sausage, skinned if necessary and thickly sliced

4 tomatoes, halved

salt and pepper

To serve

boiled rice

tomato salad

Put the onion wedges and garlic in a large roasting pan. Stir in 1 teaspoon paprika and ½ tablespoon oil.

Place the chicken on top and brush with the remaining oil. Sprinkle with the remaining paprika and season to taste with salt and pepper.

Insert a couple of rosemary sprigs into the chicken cavity and roast the chicken on the lower rack of the halogen oven at 400°F (200°C) for 30 minutes.

Transfer the chicken to a plate and add the peppers, chorizo, and tomato halves to the roasting pan. Stir to combine, then put the chicken on top of the vegetables. Cook for an additional 25–30 minutes or until the chicken is cooked through and the juices run clear.

Serve with the vegetables in the roasting pan, plain boiled rice, and a tomato salad.

Serves **4**   Preparation time **20 minutes**   Cooking time **18-20 minutes**

chicken in prosciutto

4 boneless, skinless chicken breasts, each 3½-4 oz

½ cup cream cheese with herbs

8 slices of prosciutto

6-8 vine-ripened tomatoes

To serve

arugula leaves

new potatoes

Use a sharp knife to cut a pocket in each chicken breast by slicing down one of the long sides but not cutting right through. Fill each pocket with a quarter of the cream cheese and wrap each chicken breast with 2 slices of prosciutto.

Transfer the chicken to a casserole dish and cover with foil. Transfer the casserole to the lower rack of the halogen oven and cook at 400°F (200°C) for 18-20 minutes or until the chicken is cooked through and the juices run clear.

After 10 minutes add the tomatoes to the oven so that they cook for 8-10 minutes.

Serve the chicken and tomatoes on a bed of arugula leaves with new potatoes.

Serves **4**   Preparation time **10 minutes**   Cooking time **18-20 minutes**

chicken with tomatoes

4 boneless, skinless chicken
breasts, each 5-6 oz

½ cup cream cheese with
garlic or herbs

1 heaping teaspoon
sun-dried tomato paste

To serve

Baked Potatoes (see
page 122)

green salad

Use a sharp knife to cut each chicken breast in half
horizontally but not all the way through. Open out the
breasts, spread with the cream cheese and then close
together. Cover the top of each piece of chicken with
tomato paste.

Transfer the chicken to a casserole dish. Put the
casserole on the lower rack of the halogen oven and
cook at 400°F (200°C) for 18-20 minutes or until the
chicken is lightly browned and cooked through. You
may need to cover the top with foil to make sure the
chicken does not burn.

Serve with baked potatoes and a green salad.

chicken & cranberry bites

12 oz prepared puff pastry

⅔ cup cream cheese

½ cup cranberry sauce

8 oz cooked chicken or turkey, chopped

sour cream, to serve

Cut the pastry into 24 squares and arrange them on a nonstick baking sheet. You will probably have to work in 2 batches.

Spoon a little cream cheese on to each square and add some cranberry sauce and a few chicken or turkey pieces.

Put the baking sheet on the lower rack of the halogen oven and cook at 320°F (160°C) for 10-12 minutes or until the pastry is golden-brown.

Remove the bites from the oven and let cool for a few minutes before serving with sour cream to dip.

pork

Serves 4–6   Preparation time **15 minutes**   Cooking time **1 hour**

roast pork with crackling

1¾ lb boneless loin of pork joint

vegetable oil, for brushing

salt

To serve

Roasted Potatoes (see page 124)

carrots

Cauliflower Cheese (see page 127)

Pat the pork dry with kitchen paper and use a sharp knife to score it in a deep crisscross pattern.

Brush with oil and sprinkle generously with salt. Place the pork in a roasting pan, transfer to the lower rack of the halogen oven, and cook at 400°F (200°C) for 1 hour.

Serve the pork with roasted potatoes, carrots, and cauliflower cheese.

Serves 6   Preparation time **10 minutes plus chilling**   Cooking time **35–40 minutes**

herbed roast pork

4 garlic cloves, roughly chopped

leaves from 4 sprigs of rosemary

1 teaspoon ground allspice

1 tablespoon olive oil

1 lb pork tenderloin

salt and pepper

To serve

Roasted Potatoes (see page 124)

seasonal vegetables

In a bowl mix together the garlic, rosemary, and allspice to make a paste. Season to taste with salt and pepper.

Rub the oil all over the pork and then rub in the paste. Cover and chill in the refrigerator for at least 30 minutes.

Transfer the seasoned pork to a baking sheet and cover with foil. Put the baking sheet on the lower rack of the halogen oven and cook at 400°F (200°C) for 35–40 minutes, removing the foil for the last 5 minutes of the cooking time.

Serve the pork with roasted potatoes and a selection of seasonal vegetables of your choice.

Serves **4**   Preparation time **5 minutes**   Cooking time **15-20 minutes**

sausage casserole

1 tablespoon oil

1 lb new potatoes, halved

8 sausages

1 onion, chopped

1 green bell pepper, cored, seeded, and diced

1½ cups ready-made tomato pasta sauce

Heat the oil in a skillet, add the potatoes and sausages, and cook over a medium heat for 5 minutes, turning the sausages from time to time so that they brown evenly. Add the onion and pepper and cook for another 5 minutes.

Transfer the mixture to a casserole dish and stir in the pasta sauce. Put the casserole dish on the lower rack of the halogen oven, cover with foil, and cook at 400°F (200°C) for 5-10 minutes. To serve, spoon onto 4 warm serving plates.

toad-in-the-hole

½ cup all-purpose flour

1 teaspoon salt

3 eggs

¾ cup milk

4 tablespoons vegetable oil

8 pork sausages

Onion gravy

2 teaspoons oil

8 oz red onions, sliced

2 rounded teaspoons all-purpose flour

2 cups vegetable stock

1 teaspoon superfine sugar

2 teaspoons Worcestershire sauce

Make the batter. Put the flour and salt in a large bowl, make a well in the center, and add the eggs. Mix in half the milk until the mixture is smooth, then add the remaining milk. Beat until fully combined and the surface is covered with tiny bubbles. Set aside to rest.

Meanwhile, put the oil and sausages in a small roasting pan. Put it on the lower rack of the halogen oven and cook at 400°F (200°C) for 10–11 minutes or until the sausages are browned.

Making sure that the oil in the roasting pan is really hot, pour the batter over the sausages. Cook, still at 400°F (200°C), for 30–40 minutes or until the batter has risen and is a deep golden-brown.

Meanwhile, make the onion gravy. Heat the oil in a skillet and cook the onions over a medium heat for about 8 minutes.

Stir in the flour and cook for an additional 1–2 minutes. Add a little of the stock at a time, stirring to make a smooth sauce, then add the remaining ingredients. Simmer for about 5 minutes.

Cut the toad-in-the-hole into 4 portions and serve with the onion gravy.

pork kebabs

3 tablespoons medium sherry

2 teaspoons five spice powder

2 teaspoons sesame oil

1 teaspoon granulated sugar

1 garlic clove, crushed

1 teaspoon ground ginger

4 teaspoons soy sauce

12 oz pork tenderloin, cut into 1 inch cubes

1 red bell pepper, cored, seeded, and cut into 1 inch pieces

1 red onion, cut into 1 inch pieces

To serve

boiled rice

scallions, finely chopped

In a small container with a lid mix together the sherry, five spice powder, sesame oil, sugar, garlic, ginger, and soy sauce and shake well.

Put the pork in a plastic food bag and add the marinade. Turn to coat each piece, then transfer to the refrigerator for at least 2 hours or overnight.

Arrange pieces of pork, pepper, and onion alternately on skewers. (Soak wooden skewers in water overnight so they do not burn.)

Place the skewers on the lower rack of the halogen oven and cook at 400°F (200°C) for 18–20 minutes or until the pork is cooked through. Serve with boiled rice mixed with some finely chopped scallions.

pork burgers

1 lb lean ground pork

1 red dessert apple, unpeeled

1 teaspoon paprika

4 sesame-seed burger buns, halved

olive oil, for brushing

bag of mixed salad leaves

5 oz blue cheese, cut into 4 slices

Put the meat in a large bowl. Core and finely dice the apple and add to the pork together with the paprika. Mix thoroughly with your hands and shape into 4 round burgers.

Cover the upper rack of the halogen oven with foil and arrange the burgers on the foil. Cook at 400°F (200°C) for 8-10 minutes, turning them halfway through the cooking time.

Brush the cut side of the burger buns with oil. Transfer the burgers to the lower rack and place the burger buns on the upper rack, cut side up, and cook for 1-2 minutes or until brown.

Put some salad leaves on the base of each burger bun, add a burger, and top with a slice of cheese.

Serves **4**   Preparation time **10 minutes**   Cooking time **14–15 minutes**

cider pork

2 red dessert apples, cored and cut into wedges
4 pork loin steaks
¾ cup hard cider
¾ cup sour cream
salt and pepper

To serve
new potatoes
seasonal vegetables

Put the apple wedges on the lower rack of the halogen oven and cook at 400°F (200°C) for 4–5 minutes. Set aside.

At the same time, season the pork steaks with salt and pepper and place them on the upper rack of the halogen oven. Cook them at 400°F (200°C) for 2–3 minutes on each side.

Pour the cider into a casserole dish, place on the lower rack of the halogen oven, and cook at 480°F (250°C) for 5 minutes or until it has reduced by half.

Reduce the heat to 400°F (200°C) and stir in the sour cream. Add the apples and pork to the casserole dish and cook, simmering, for 5 minutes, turning halfway through the cooking time, until cooked through.

Transfer to plates. Spoon the sauce over the pork and serve with new potatoes and seasonal vegetables.

stuffed pork tenderloin

7 oz pork tenderloin

½ tablespoon toasted pine nuts, roughly chopped

½ tablespoon raisins

1 tablespoon butter

3 thin slices of Serrano ham

olive oil, for brushing

salt and pepper

Roasted Potatoes (see page 124), to serve

Use a sharp knife to make a vertical incision in the pork all the way down the middle, but do not cut all the way through. Make further cuts on each side of this incision so that you can open out the loin. Season with salt and pepper and sprinkle with the pine nuts and raisins and dot with butter.

Fold over the flaps of the pork so that the filling is fully enclosed. Wrap the ham around the pork, making sure that there are no gaps. Wrap the pork tightly in plastic wrap and put it in the refrigerator for 25 minutes.

Fill a casserole dish with water, put it in the halogen oven at 480°F (250°C) and bring to a boil. Wrap the tenderloin, still in plastic wrap, in foil, add to the boiling water and poach for 8–10 minutes or until the pork is just cooked. Remove the pork from the pan, remove the foil, and hold under cold running water for 10 minutes.

Remove the plastic wrap and dry the pork thoroughly with paper towels. Brush the surface of the pork with oil, put the meat on the top rack of the halogen oven, and cook at 400°F (200°C) for 5–6 minutes to brown the surface and heat through.

Cut the pork into slices and arrange on 2 plates. Serve with roasted potatoes.

Serves **4** Preparation time **20 minutes** Cooking time **15 minutes**

barbecue ribs

⅔ cup balsamic vinegar

¼ teaspoon crushed red pepper

2½ lb pork spare ribs

Coleslaw

4 tablespoons light mayonnaise

2 tablespoons lemon juice

1 small onion, finely sliced

½ white cabbage, finely shredded

1 carrot, roughly grated

2 celery sticks, finely sliced diagonally

salt and pepper

Make the glaze. Put the balsamic vinegar and crushed pepper into a small saucepan over a high heat. Bring to a boil, reduce the heat, and simmer for about 5 minutes or until reduced by half and slightly thickened.

Make the coleslaw. Put the mayonnaise in a bowl, stir in the lemon juice, and season well with salt and pepper. Add the onion, cabbage, carrot, and celery and mix together.

Brush the glaze over the ribs and arrange them on the upper rack in the halogen oven. Cook at 400°F (200°C) for 10 minutes. Arrange the cooked ribs on 4 plates and serve with the coleslaw.

A halogen oven with baking racks and handle

Removing a cooking rack from an oven using the handles

Drying a washed bowl with a clean cloth

Paprika Chicken (see page 18)

Serves 4   Preparation time **15 minutes**   Cooking time **20-25 minutes**

roasted pork with orange

4 thick slices of white bread, crusts removed

juice and finely grated zest of 1 orange

4 sprigs of thyme

2 pork tenderloin fillets, each about 14½ oz

2 teaspoons cornstarch

1¼ cups vegetable or chicken stock

Roasted Potatoes (see page 124), to serve

Whizz the bread in a food processor to make bread crumbs. Transfer to a bowl and mix with the orange zest and thyme.

Lay each piece of pork on a board and use a sharp knife to make a deep slit along the length to create a pocket. Fill the pockets with the bread crumb mixture and secure with toothpicks.

Place the pork in a roasting pan and transfer to the lower rack of the halogen oven. Cook at 400°F (200°C) for 15-20 minutes or until cooked through. Remove the pork from the oven, transfer to a plate, and cover with foil.

In a small bowl mix the orange juice with the cornstarch to make a smooth paste. Put the paste in the roasting pan with the pork juices and heat on the stovetop over a high heat. Add the stock and bring to a boil, stirring, then simmer for 3-4 minutes until thickened.

Remove the toothpicks from the pork and slice the meat onto 4 plates. Drizzle over the sauce and serve with roasted potatoes.

lamb

Serves 4 Preparation time **10 minutes** Cooking time **30-35 minutes**

rack of lamb

6 tablespoons honey

3 tablespoons light soy sauce

2 tablespoons English mustard

2 tablespoons chopped mint

2 x 6-bone lean racks of lamb

salt and pepper

To serve

Roasted Potatoes (see page 124)

green beans

carrots

In a bowl mix together the honey, soy sauce, mustard, and mint.

Put the racks of lamb, fat side up, on a cutting board. Season to taste on both sides with salt and pepper and brush on both sides with the honey mixture. Transfer to a foil-lined baking sheet.

Put the racks of lamb on the lower rack of the halogen oven and cook at 400°F (200°C) for 30-35 minutes. Remember to cover the racks of lamb with foil if they look as if they are burning.

Divide the lamb and transfer to 4 plates. Serve with roasted potatoes, green beans, and carrots.

sticky chops

6 lamb chops, each 2-2½ oz

green salad, to serve

Sticky marinade

2 tablespoons white wine vinegar

½ teaspoon ground nutmeg

2 garlic cloves, crushed

1 tablespoon light brown sugar

4 tablespoons plum jelly

5 tablespoons tomato ketchup

1 tablespoon soy sauce (optional)

1 tablespoon sweet chili sauce (optional)

salt and pepper

In a large, nonmetallic bowl mix together all the ingredients for the marinade, making sure they are thoroughly combined.

Add the chops to the bowl and turn them to coat completely in the marinade. Cover and transfer to the refrigerator for at least 2 hours or overnight.

Put the chops on the upper rack in the halogen oven and cook at 400°F (200°C) for 10-15 minutes, turning occasionally. Serve with a green salad.

lamb shanks

olive oil, for braising

2 lamb shanks

1 leek, roughly chopped

2 celery sticks, roughly chopped

2 carrots, roughly chopped

2 onions, roughly chopped

1 whole head of garlic, cloves separated but unpeeled

1½ cups red wine

2½ cups chicken stock

Pour olive oil into a casserole dish to a depth of ½ inch and heat on the stovetop over a high heat until the oil is sizzling. Add the lamb shanks and cook, turning occasionally, until brown.

Remove the lamb shanks from the casserole with a slotted spoon and add the leek, celery, carrots, onions, and garlic. Cook for 10–12 minutes or until they begin to soften.

Return the lamb to the casserole, arranging the shanks on top of the vegetables. Add the red wine and chicken stock and bring to a boil.

Transfer the casserole dish to the lower rack of the halogen oven, cover with foil, and cook at 350°F (180°C) for 1 hour. Check that the meat is falling off the bone; if not, cook for an additional 20 minutes.

Serve the lamb with the vegetables and with the cooking juices poured over the top.

curried lamb kebabs

1 lb lean ground lamb

2 teaspoons ground cumin

2 teaspoons ground turmeric

1 tablespoon sunflower oil

2 garlic cloves, crushed

½ teaspoon superfine sugar

boiled rice, to serve

Dip

¾ cup whole milk yogurt

4 tablespoons mint jelly

Put the meat in a large bowl. Add the cumin, turmeric, oil, garlic, and sugar and mix well. Cover and leave in the refrigerator for 2 hours or overnight.

Use the spicy meat mixture to form 10-12 sausages around the skewers. Remember to soak wooden skewers in water before use so that they do not burn during cooking.

Arrange the kebabs on the upper rack of the halogen oven and cook at 400°F (200°C) for 12-15 minutes.

Meanwhile, mix together the yogurt and mint jelly in a bowl. Serve the skewers with the dip and accompanied by boiled rice.

lamb hotpot

1 lb lean ground lamb

1½ cups sliced mushrooms

2 cups hot lamb stock

2 tablespoons instant gravy mix

1 tablespoon thyme leaves

2 leeks, finely sliced

2 oz Lancashire cheese, grated

1½ lb potatoes, sliced

melted butter

salt and pepper

In a large, nonstick skillet over a medium heat dry-fry the lamb with the mushrooms for 4–5 minutes until evenly browned. Add the stock, gravy mix, and thyme and cook for 2–3 minutes more until thickened. Season to taste with salt and pepper and transfer to a casserole dish.

Cover the lamb with the leeks and cheese and then layer the potatoes over the top. Brush the potatoes with melted butter and cover with foil.

Place the casserole dish on the lower rack of the halogen oven and cook at 350°F (180°C) for 25 minutes, removing the foil for the last 5–10 minutes to allow the potatoes to brown.

lamb **mixed grill**

4 lamb loin chops

4 beef sausages

2 tomatoes, halved

2 large mushrooms

2 tablespoons butter

salt and pepper

Chunky Fries (see page 123), to serve

Arrange the chops, sausages, tomatoes, and mushrooms on a baking sheet. Put some of the butter on each mushroom. Season to taste with salt and pepper.

Put the baking sheet on the lower rack of the halogen oven and cook at 400°F (200°C) for 10–15 minutes, turning the chops and sausages about halfway through the cooking time.

Transfer the mixed grill to 2 warm plates and serve with homemade fries.

spicy lamb meatballs

1 lb ground lamb

1 small onion, finely chopped

¼ teaspoon ground allspice

¼ teaspoon juniper berries, crushed

1 sprig of thyme, leaves roughly chopped

2 tablespoons currants

3 tablespoons olive oil

tagliatelle, to serve

Put the lamb in a large bowl and add the onion, allspice, juniper berries, thyme, and currants. Mix the ingredients together thoroughly and then form the mixture into 15–20 small balls, each about the size of a golf ball.

Brush the bottom of a casserole dish with oil and arrange the meatballs in the dish. Place on the lower rack of the halogen oven and cook at 400°F (200°C) for 4–5 minutes.

Serve with pasta, such as tagliatelle, cooked according to the instructions on the package.

Serves 6   Preparation time **15 minutes**   Cooking time **30–40 minutes**

lamb with spicy sausage

1 lb lean lamb, cut into 1 inch cubes

2 tablespoons all-purpose flour seasoned with salt and pepper

2 tablespoons olive oil

4 oz chorizo or spicy paprika sausage, skinned and cut into large pieces

1 red onion, finely chopped

2 garlic cloves, crushed

1¼ cups hot lamb stock

⅔ cup red wine

13¼ oz can black-eye peas or lima beans, rinsed and drained

Sweet Potato Wedges (see page 123), to serve

Coat the lamb in the seasoned flour.

Heat the oil in a large, nonstick skillet and cook the lamb and chorizo over a medium heat for 3–4 minutes or until brown. Transfer to a large, ovenproof casserole dish; the casserole should hold about 3 quarts but check first that it will fit inside your halogen oven.

In the same skillet cook the onions and garlic until soft. Transfer to the casserole together with the stock and wine.

Cook on the lower rack of the halogen oven at 400°F (200°C) for 22–25 minutes, stirring occasionally. About 10 minutes before the end of the cooking time add the beans and reduce the heat to 320°F (160°C).

Serve the lamb with sweet potato wedges.

Serves **6**   Preparation time **20 minutes**   Cooking time **29 minutes**

lamb stew

2 lb lean boneless lamb shoulder, cubed

2 bay leaves

4 sprigs of thyme

1 onion, quartered

1 leek, roughly chopped

3 garlic cloves, crushed

5 cups cold water

8 oz baby carrots

8 oz baby turnips

8 oz baby onions or shallots

8 oz small leeks

¾ cup white wine (dry or medium)

¾ cup hot lamb stock

8 oz green beans, trimmed

1⅓ cups peas

salt and pepper

mashed potato, to serve

Place the lamb in a roasting pan with the bay leaves, thyme, onion, leek, garlic, and water. Season to taste with salt and pepper and cover with foil.

Put the roasting pan on the lower rack of the halogen oven and cook at 400°F (200°C) for 15 minutes.

Transfer the lamb to a large casserole dish and strain the vegetable juices over the meat, discarding the vegetables and herbs.

Add the carrots, turnips, onions or shallots, leeks, white wine, and stock to the lamb. Place the casserole on the lower rack of the halogen oven and cook at 480°F (250°C) for 10 minutes.

Add the green beans to the casserole and cook for 2 minutes more. Add the peas and cook for another 2 minutes or until the vegetables are cooked. Serve with mashed potato.

Serves 6   Preparation time **20 minutes**   Cooking time **30-37 minutes**

lamb ragout

1 tablespoon olive oil

1 lb 6 oz boneless lamb shoulder, leg, or neck fillet, cut into 1 inch cubes

grated zest of 1 lemon

2 garlic cloves, crushed

6 scallions, finely chopped

⅔ cup hard cider or white wine

2½ cups hot lamb or vegetable stock

2 bay leaves

½ cup corn kernels

3 oz cauliflower florets

2 zucchini, roughly chopped

3 oz sugar snap peas

small handful of chopped mint leaves

salt and pepper

new potatoes, to serve

Heat the oil in a large ovenproof casserole dish, add the lamb, lemon zest, and garlic and cook, stirring occasionally, over a medium heat for 4-5 minutes until brown. Transfer to a plate.

Add the scallions to the same casserole dish and cook for 1-2 minutes until soft. Return the lamb to the casserole and add the cider or wine, hot stock, and bay leaves.

Transfer the casserole to the lower rack of the halogen oven and cook at 400°F (200°C) for 20 minutes.

Add the corn, cauliflower, and zucchini and cook for an additional 5-10 minutes.

Season to taste with salt and pepper, stir through the sugar snap peas and mint, and serve immediately with new potatoes.

beef

traditional roast beef

2½ lb lean boneless rump roast

3 red onions, cut into wedges

10 garlic cloves, unpeeled

To serve

Roasted Potatoes (see page 124)

seasonal vegetables

Put the beef on a small baking sheet on the upper rack in the halogen oven and cook at 400°F (200°C) for 45–50 minutes.

After 20 minutes add the red onions and garlic to the base of the oven and place the beef on top of the vegetables.

Remove the beef from the oven and let it rest for 5–10 minutes then serve with the onions and garlic, roasted potatoes, and seasonal vegetables.

Pork Kebabs (see page 28)

Cooking racks of lamb in a halogen oven

Rack of Lamb (see page 40)

Lamb Ragout (see page 49)

spicy steaks

1 lb 6 oz lean thin steaks

Spicy marinade

4 garlic cloves, finely chopped

1 red chili, seeded and finely chopped

juice of 1 orange

juice of 1 lemon

2 tablespoons chopped flat leaf parsley

3 tablespoons olive oil

salt and pepper

To serve

green salad

Chunky Fries (see page 123)

Make the marinade. Mix together all the ingredients in a large, nonmetallic dish. Add the steaks to the mixture, turning them to coat both sides. Cover and refrigerate for at least 1 hour.

Place the steaks directly on the upper rack of the halogen oven and cook at 400°F (200°C) for 3–4 minutes (medium rare), 5–6 minutes (medium) and 10 minutes or more for well done.

Serve the steaks with homemade fries and a fresh green salad.

beef stew with dumplings

1 tablespoon vegetable oil

450 g (14½ oz) lean braising steak, cubed

2 celery sticks, chopped

6 baby carrots, left whole

½ small rutabaga, chopped

2 parsnips, chopped

2½ cups hot beef stock

1 tablespoon Worcestershire sauce

2 tablespoons instant gravy mix

Dumplings

1 cup self-rising flour

½ cup suet

1 tablespoon wholegrain mustard

5 tablespoons water

To serve

carrots

broccoli

Heat the oil in a skillet and cook the braising steak for 4-5 minutes until browned on all sides.

Transfer the meat to a casserole dish and add the celery, carrots, rutabaga, and parsnips. Pour over the stock and stir in the Worcestershire sauce.

Cover the casserole with foil, place on the lower rack of the halogen oven, and cook at 320°F (160°C) for 40 minutes or until the beef is tender.

Meanwhile, make the dumplings. Mix together the flour, suet, mustard, and water in a bowl to form a smooth dough. Divide it into 8 equal pieces and form them into balls.

After the beef has been cooking for 20 minutes remove the casserole from the oven. Remove the foil and stir in the gravy mix and arrange the dumplings on top.

Return the casserole dish, uncovered, to the halogen oven and cook at 400°F (200°C) for the remaining 20 minutes. Serve with buttered carrots and broccoli.

red pepper burgers

1 lb lean ground beef

1 small onion, finely grated

1 garlic clove, crushed

1 small red bell pepper, seeded and finely diced

½ teaspoon dried mixed herbs

2 tablespoons sweet chili sauce

½–1 cup fresh bread crumbs

1 egg, beaten

1 tablespoon sunflower or vegetable oil

salt and pepper

To serve

burger buns

salad leaves

tomato slices

red onion slices

mayonnaise

Put the beef in a large bowl and combine it with the onion, garlic, red pepper, herbs, sweet chili sauce, and bread crumbs. Season to taste with salt and pepper and mix in the egg. Mix together thoroughly, cover, and refrigerate for 30 minutes.

Shape the mixture into 4-6 even-sized burgers. Brush each burger with oil and cook on the upper rack of the halogen oven at 400°F (200°C) for 10-11 minutes.

Serve the burgers in the split buns with salad leaves, slices of tomato and red onion, and mayonnaise.

Serves 6 Preparation time **20 minutes** Cooking time **17-22 minutes**

beef-stuffed peppers

3 large red bell peppers

1 tablespoon olive oil

12 oz lean ground beef

¾ cup pureed tomatoes

½ small onion, finely chopped

2 garlic cloves, finely chopped

1 celery stick, finely chopped

1 tablespoon chopped oregano

2 oz reduced-fat cheese, grated

salt and pepper

sprigs of thyme, to garnish

Cut the peppers in half at the longest point and remove the cores and seeds. Place them on a baking sheet and brush with oil. Put the baking sheet on the lower rack of the halogen oven and roast at 400°F (200°C) for 10 minutes.

Meanwhile, put the meat in a large skillet and dry-fry over a medium heat until it is brown. Drain away any juices and transfer the beef to a bowl.

Add the pureed tomatoes, onion, garlic, celery, and oregano and season to taste with salt and pepper. Mix together thoroughly.

Remove the peppers from the halogen oven and divide the filling among them. Place the peppers on the lower rack, cover with foil, and cook at 320°F (160°C) for an additional 5-10 minutes.

Remove the foil from the peppers, sprinkle with the cheese, and return the peppers to the oven for another 2 minutes or until the cheese has melted. Serve immediately, garnished with thyme sprigs.

chili roast beef

3-4 lb lean beef joint
salt and pepper

Marinade

1 teaspoon crushed red pepper

2 garlic cloves, crushed

1 tablespoon finely chopped fresh ginger root

3 tablespoons chopped chives

2 tablespoons sherry vinegar

To serve

Dauphinoise Potatoes (see page 122)

seasonal vegetables

Put the beef on a cutting board and lightly score the surface with a sharp knife.

Transfer the meat to a nonmetallic dish and season to taste with salt and pepper.

Make the marinade. Mix together all the ingredients and rub the mixture all over the joint. Cover and marinate in the refrigerator for 2 hours or overnight.

Take the joint out of the refrigerator and discard any excess marinade. Put the beef on the lower rack of the halogen oven and cook at 400°F (200°C) for 45-50 minutes, covering the meat with foil if it looks as if it is drying out.

Remove the beef from the oven and let it rest for about 10 minutes then slice and serve with dauphinoise potatoes and seasonal vegetables.

steak & kidney pies

1 tablespoon sunflower oil

1 lb lean braising or stewing steak, cubed

1 onion, sliced

4 oz chestnut mushrooms, quartered

8 oz ox kidney, cored, trimmed, and cut into small chunks

1 tablespoon all-purpose flour

2 cups hot beef stock

¾ cup English beer

1 lb short crust pastry (thawed if frozen)

1 egg, beaten

salt and pepper

To serve

peas

Chunky Fries (see page 123)

Heat the oil in a large skillet and cook the beef over a medium heat for 3-4 minutes until brown on all sides.

Add the onion and mushrooms to the pan and cook for an additional 4-5 minutes until browned. Add the kidneys and cook for 1-2 minutes. Sprinkle with the flour.

Transfer the meat and vegetables to a casserole dish and add the stock and beer. Season to taste with salt and pepper. Put the casserole on the lower rack of the halogen oven, cover with foil, and cook at 400°F (200°C) for 45-50 minutes or until the meat is tender. Spoon the cooked mixture into 2 individual pie dishes.

Roll out the pastry and cut out 2 lids slightly larger than each dish. Place the pastry lid on top of the meat filling, dampening the edges of each dish. Trim away the excess pastry and press the edges to seal. Brush the tops with egg and cook the pies at 450°F (230°C) for 20-25 minutes or until the pastry is golden, covering the pastry for the first 10-15 minutes so that it does not burn.

Divide the pies in half and serve with peas and homemade fries.

chili

1 tablespoon oil

2 onions, finely chopped

2 large garlic cloves, crushed

1½ lb lean ground beef

⅔ cup red wine

2 x 13 oz cans chopped tomatoes

2–3 tablespoons tomato paste

2 teaspoons crushed red pepper, plus extra to serve

1–2 tablespoons sweet chili sauce

2 teaspoons ground cumin

2 teaspoons ground coriander

1 teaspoon ground ginger

1–2 bay leaves

2 tablespoons good quality cocoa powder

1 beef bouillon cube

2 x 13 oz cans red kidney beans, rinsed and drained

salt and pepper

boiled rice, to serve

Heat the oil in a large, nonstick skillet and cook the onions and garlic over a medium heat for 1–2 minutes.

Add the beef and cook for a few minutes until brown. Add the wine and cook for an additional 2–3 minutes.

Transfer the meat mixture to a casserole dish and stir in the tomatoes, tomato paste, crushed pepper, sweet chili sauce, spices, bay leaves, and cocoa powder. Crumble over the bouillon cube and season to taste with salt and pepper. Stir to mix.

Put the casserole dish in the halogen oven and cook at 400°F (200°C) for 30 minutes. Add the red kidney beans and cook for 10 minutes more.

Serve with plain boiled rice and a sprinkling of crushed red pepper.

steak with tangy sauce

2 sirloin, porterhouse,
rib-eye or tenderloin steaks

2 teaspoons olive oil

green salad, to serve

Tangy sauce

2 tablespoons olive oil

2 garlic cloves, finely
chopped

6 tablespoons sweet sherry

6 tablespoons red wine

6 tablespoons hot beef
stock or water

1 tablespoon tomato paste

pinch of crushed red pepper
(optional)

2 tablespoons chopped
chives

salt and pepper

Make the sauce. Heat the oil in a skillet, add the garlic, and cook over a medium heat until soft. Add the sherry and wine, bring to a boil, reduce the heat and cook, stirring, for 10-15 minutes until the sauce has thickened.

Stir in the stock or water, tomato paste and crushed pepper, if using. Season to taste with salt and pepper. Add the chives, increase the heat, and boil the sauce for a couple of minutes to thicken.

Meanwhile, put the steaks on the upper rack of the halogen oven and brush with a little oil. Cook at 400°F (200°C) for 15 minutes for a well-done steak, reducing the time if you prefer your meat less well done.

Serve the steaks with a little of the sauce poured over and a crisp green salad.

thai beef curry

1¼ cups coconut milk

1¼ cups water

2 tablespoons Thai red curry paste

1 stalk of lemon grass, sliced thinly

4 dried or fresh kaffir lime leaves

1 tablespoon lime juice

1 tablespoon Thai fish sauce (nam pla)

1 lb lean sirloin steak, trimmed of any fat and thinly sliced

8 oz shallots, sliced

1 cup thinly sliced carrots

6 oz sugar snap peas

10 cherry tomatoes, halved

3 tablespoons chopped cilantro

Pilau Rice (see page 125), to serve

Pour the coconut milk and water into a large saucepan. Add the curry paste, lemon grass, kaffir lime leaves, lime juice, and fish sauce, bring to a boil and boil quickly for 2 minutes.

Transfer the coconut milk mixture to a casserole dish and add the meat and shallots. Place on the upper rack of the halogen oven and cook at 400°F (200°C) for 10 minutes.

Add the carrots and sugar snap peas to the curry and cook for another 8-10 minutes. Stir in the tomatoes and cilantro and cook for 2 minutes more.

Serve the curry with pilau rice.

fish & seafood

salmon fishcakes

1½ lb potatoes, cut into large chunks

2 tablespoons butter

7½ oz can red salmon, drained

2 tablespoons chopped parsley

1 egg, beaten

1 tablespoon flour

salt and pepper

To serve

lettuce leaves

lemon wedges

Cook the potatoes in a large saucepan of boiling water for 10–12 minutes or until they are tender. Drain and return to the pan.

Mash the potatoes with the butter and stir in the salmon and parsley. Season to taste with salt and pepper and mix with sufficient egg for the mixture to bind together. Divide the mixture into 12 equal portions and shape them into patties.

Cover each fishcake in a light coating of flour and place them on the lower rack of the halogen oven. Cook at 480°F (250°C) for 8–10 minutes or until golden-brown, covering them with foil for the first 5 minutes so that they don't burn.

Serve the fishcakes on a bed of crisp lettuce with lemon wedges to squeeze over.

mushroom-stuffed plaice

4 whole plaice

1 tablespoon oil

1 onion, finely chopped

1 garlic clove, crushed

1½ cups brown bread crumbs

4 oz mushrooms, finely chopped

1 tomato, peeled and chopped

1 teaspoon chopped marjoram

2 teaspoons chopped parsley

dash of Worcestershire sauce

sprigs of watercress, to garnish

To serve

broiled tomatoes

broiled mushrooms

Put the fish, skin side down, on a board. Use a sharp knife to cut 2 pockets into the sides of each fish. Do this by making a cut down the backbone. On one half cut two-thirds of the way around to form a pocket; repeat on the other half.

Make the mushroom filling. Heat the oil in a large skillet. Add the onion, garlic, and bread crumbs and fry over a medium heat until the bread crumbs are crisp. Stir in the mushrooms, tomato, herbs, and Worcestershire sauce and fry for 2 more minutes.

Stuff the fish with the filling, arrange them in a buttered ovenproof dish, and cover with foil. Cook on the upper rack of the halogen oven at 480°F (250°C) for 8-10 minutes.

Transfer the fish to serving plates and garnish with the watercress. Serve immediately with broiled tomatoes and mushrooms.

crusty salmon

4 salmon fillets, each about 4 oz

2 tablespoons olive oil

1 cup rolled oats

zest of 1 large lemon

3 tablespoons chopped herbs, such as parsley or dill

salt and pepper

To serve

new potatoes

green salad

Brush the salmon all over with oil.

Combine the oats, lemon zest, and herbs in a bowl and season to taste with salt and pepper.

Tip the oat mixture onto a plate. Dip the rounded surface of each salmon fillet into the oat mixture and transfer to a small baking sheet. Cook on the upper rack of the halogen oven at 480°F (250°C) for 8-10 minutes.

Serve the salmon immediately with new potatoes and a crisp green salad.

Serves **2**   Preparation time **10 minutes**   Cooking time **8–10 minutes**

honey & sesame salmon

1 tablespoon honey

2 tablespoons soy sauce

2 salmon fillets, each about 5 oz

2 tablespoons chopped scallions

2 tablespoons sesame seeds

To serve

new potatoes

arugula leaves

In a bowl mix together the honey and soy sauce. Drizzle the honey mixture over the salmon fillet.

Sprinkle the salmon with chopped scallions and roll them in sesame seeds. Transfer them, skin side down, to a foil-lined baking sheet.

Cook the salmon on the upper rack of the halogen oven at 480°F (250°C) for 8–10 minutes.

Serve immediately with new potatoes and a peppery arugula salad.

Serves 4 Preparation time **15 minutes** Cooking time **8 minutes**

tuna with salsa

4 tuna steaks, each
4-5 oz

1 tablespoon olive oil

salt and pepper

Salsa

2 ripe nectarines or peaches

1 small red onion, finely
diced

1 green chili, seeded and
finely chopped

2 tablespoons chopped
mint

2 tablespoons chopped basil

zest and juice of 1 lime

1 teaspoon olive oil

To serve

green salad

lime wedges

Make the salsa. Remove the skins and pits from the peaches or nectarines. Chop the flesh, put the pieces in a bowl, and mix in the onion, chili, herbs, lime zest and juice, and oil. Set aside.

Brush the tuna with oil and season to taste with salt and pepper.

Place 2 of the tuna steaks on the upper rack of the halogen oven and cook at 480°F (250°C) for 2 minutes each side. Repeat with the remaining tuna.

Serve with green salad, the salsa, and lime wedges to squeeze over the fish.

tuna pasta bake

2 x 6¼ oz cans tuna in brine

1 tablespoon olive oil, plus extra for greasing

4 scallions or 1 small onion, finely chopped

10 oz small pasta shapes, such as penne

2½ cups milk

¼ cup all-purpose flour

2 tablespoons butter

1 cup grated sharp cheddar cheese

1 teaspoon mustard

½ teaspoon lemon juice

Garlic bread

2 small, part-baked baguettes

1 garlic clove, halved

2 tablespoons butter

Drain the tuna and flake the flesh into a bowl.

Heat the oil in a skillet and cook the scallions or onion over a medium heat for a couple of minutes to soften.

Meanwhile, cook the pasta in a large saucepan of boiling water according to the instructions on the package. Drain and set aside.

Put the milk, flour, and butter in a small saucepan and beat constantly over a medium heat until the sauce begins to boil and thicken. Turn down the heat to its lowest and let the sauce cook very gently for 2 minutes. Add about ¾ cup grated cheese and the lemon juice and mustard.

Mix the pasta with the scallions or onion, tuna, and cheese sauce and pour into a lightly oiled 5–6 cup casserole dish.

Sprinkle with the remaining cheese and bake on the lower rack of the halogen oven at 400°F (200°C) for about 20 minutes or until the top is golden.

Meanwhile, make garlic bread by cutting each baguette in half lengthwise. Rub the cut surfaces with garlic and spread with butter. Bake on the upper rack of the halogen oven at 200° for 6-8 minutes.

Spoon the pasta bake onto warm plates and serve with chunks of garlic bread.

baked halibut

1 lb small waxy new potatoes, thinly sliced

2 tablespoons olive oil, plus extra for drizzling

1 lb frozen Ratatouille (see page 129)

1 red chili, seeded and finely chopped or a generous pinch of crushed red pepper

4 halibut steaks, each about 7 oz

1 lemon, sliced

salt and pepper

bread and butter, to serve

Put the potatoes in a large bowl. Pour over the oil and season to taste with salt and pepper. Turn to coat the slices evenly.

Arrange the potato slices in layers on a large baking sheet, place on the lower rack of the halogen oven, and cook at 480°F (250°C) for 20-25 minutes or until turning golden.

Spoon the frozen ratatouille over the potatoes and sprinkle with the chili. Put the halibut on top of the ratatouille and arrange the lemon slices over the fish.

Season to taste with salt and pepper and cook on the upper rack of the halogen oven at 480°F (250°C) for 8-10 minutes or until the fish is cooked through. Serve with chunky bread and butter.

tandoori shrimp

4 tablespoons plain yogurt

2 tablespoons tandoori curry paste

1 lb large uncooked peeled shrimp

½ cup basmati rice

Raita

½ cucumber

½ cup plain yogurt

a handful of chopped mint leaves

salt and pepper

To garnish

sprigs of mint

lime wedges (optional)

In a bowl mix together the yogurt and curry paste. Add the shrimp and turn to coat thoroughly.

Arrange the shrimp in a single layer on a foil-covered baking sheet and pour over any remaining marinade. Place the shrimp on the upper rack of the halogen oven and cook at 480°F (250°C) for 4–5 minutes.

Meanwhile, cook the rice according to the instructions on the package.

Make the raita. Use a vegetable peeler to cut long, thin strips from the cucumber and pat them dry on paper towels. Transfer the cucumber to a bowl and add the yogurt and mint. Season to taste with salt and pepper and mix together.

Serve the shrimp, garnished with mint sprigs and lime wedges, if desired, and accompanied with the rice and raita.

shrimp & salmon pie

1¼ lb salmon fillet, skinned and cut into 1 inch pieces

8 oz uncooked peeled shrimp

1 cup ready-made parsley sauce

2-3 large handfuls of baby spinach leaves, washed

6 oz puff pastry

1 egg, beaten

salt and pepper

Put the salmon and shrimp in a casserole dish. Pour the sauce into the casserole and mix gently to combine. Season to taste with salt and pepper.

Transfer the casserole dish to the upper rack of the halogen oven and cook at 480°F (250°C) until just bubbling. Reduce the heat to 400°F (200°C) and cook for an additional 8-10 minutes or until the fish is cooked through.

Add the spinach and cook for a couple of minutes until the leaves have begun to wilt.

Meanwhile, roll out the pastry and cut it into 4 equal pieces. Place these on a small nonstick baking sheet and use a knife to score each with a crisscross pattern. Brush with a little egg. Move the fish to the lower rack and cook the pastry on the upper rack for 5-10 minutes or until well risen and golden, covering it with foil for the first 5 minutes so that it doesn't burn.

Spoon the fish mixture onto 4 plates and serve each one topped with a piece of pastry.

Serves **4**   Preparation time **10 minutes**   Cooking time **22 minutes**

haddock & broccoli pie

12 oz broccoli, divided into florets

1 lb smoked haddock, cut into chunks

1 package of parsley sauce mix

4 sheets of phyllo dough (thawed if frozen)

¼ cup butter, melted

To serve

Roasted Potatoes (see page 124)

peas

Bring a large saucepan of lightly salted water to a boil. Add the broccoli to the water to blanch it, remove it, drain and refresh under cold water. Drain again.

Put the broccoli and haddock in the base of a casserole dish. Make up the sauce according to the instructions on the package and spoon over enough to cover the broccoli and haddock.

Brush a sheet of phyllo dough with melted butter. Tear it into 4 strips and drape them over the fish and broccoli. Repeat with the other 3 sheets of dough until the fish and broccoli are completely covered. (You may not need to use all the dough.)

Cover the pie with foil and cook in the halogen oven at 480°F (250°C) for about 15 minutes. Remove the foil and cook for an additional 5 minutes or until the pastry is golden and the filling begins to bubble.

Transfer the pie to 4 serving plates and serve with roasted potatoes and peas.

pasta & pizzas

Serves **2** Preparation time **10 minutes** Cooking time **about 10 minutes**

lamb pasta

8 oz lamb leg steaks

2 oz asparagus, sliced

1 zucchini, sliced

⅔ cup peas

5 oz pasta ribbons

1 tablepoon olive oil

1 tablespoon mint sauce

2 tablespoons honey

sprigs of mint, to garnish

Cut the lamb into thin strips and put the meat in a casserole dish. Cook on the lower rack of the halogen oven at 400°F (200°C) for 3-4 minutes or until the meat has browned.

Add the asparagus, zucchini, and peas to the casserole dish and cook for another 3-4 minutes.

Meanwhile, cook the pasta in boiling water according to the instructions on the package. Drain and mix together the oil, mint sauce, and honey and add to the casserole dish.

Combine the lamb, pasta, and vegetables and heat for a couple of minutes more, still on the lower rack.

Serve the pasta in warm bowls, garnished with mint sprigs.

Serves 4   Preparation time **20 minutes**   Cooking time **45–50 minutes**

chili pasta bake

1 lb lean ground beef

1 onion, finely chopped

2 celery sticks, finely chopped

1 small red chili, seeded and finely chopped

7 oz dried pasta shapes

5 oz chestnut mushrooms, sliced

2 large sprigs of thyme, roughly chopped

2 tablespoons sweet sherry

2 oz mozzarella cheese, grated

¼ cup grated Parmesan cheese

2 cups hot beef gravy

2 tablespoons chopped flat leaf parsley, to garnish

salt and pepper

To serve

green salad

Garlic Bread (see page 73)

Put the beef, onion, celery, and chili in a large, nonstick skillet and dry-fry over a medium heat until brown.

Meanwhile, cook the pasta according to the instructions on the package. Drain and set aside.

Add the mushrooms, thyme, and sherry to the beef and season to taste with salt and pepper.

Mix together the mozzarella and Parmesan.

Transfer the beef mixture to a casserole dish and stir in the gravy. Put the casserole on the lower rack of the halogen oven and cook at 400°F (200°C) for 10 minutes.

Combine the pasta with the beef, add half the cheese mixture, and stir to mix. Sprinkle with the remaining cheese and cook on the lower rack at 350°F (180°C) for another 10–15 minutes.

Serve immediately with a crisp green salad and chunks of warm garlic bread.

pork pasta with lemon

1 lb small pasta shapes

6 pork sausages

grated zest and juice of 1 lemon

pinch of crushed red pepper

¾ cup half-fat sour cream

½ cup grated Parmesan cheese, to serve

Cook the pasta according to the instructions on the package. Drain thoroughly.

Meanwhile, split the skins of the sausages and transfer the meat to a casserole dish, discarding the skins and breaking up the meat with a fork.

Cook the sausagemeat on the lower rack of the halogen oven at 480°F (250°C) for 8-10 minutes or until golden and crispy.

Add the lemon zest, lemon juice (to taste), crushed pepper, and the sour cream, stir, and cook for couple of minutes more until the sauce is bubbling.

Toss the pasta and meat together to combine and serve with grated Parmesan.

Serves 4   Preparation time **10 minutes**   Cooking time **17–20 minutes**

sausage pasta bake

8 pork and herb sausages, cut into chunks

1½ cups ready-made tomato and roasted vegetables pasta sauce

12 oz dried penne pasta

handful of torn basil leaves

5 oz mozzarella cheese, drained and diced

salt and pepper

½ cup grated Parmesan cheese, to serve

Cook the sausage chunks on the upper rack of the halogen oven at 400°F (200°C) for 4–5 minutes or until brown.

Transfer the sausage to a casserole dish and add the pasta sauce. Cook on the lower rack of the halogen oven at 400°F (200°C) for 10 minutes. Season to taste with salt and pepper.

Meanwhile, cook the pasta according to the instructions on the package. Drain thoroughly and add to the casserole dish.

Sprinkle the mozzarella over the top of the pasta mixture and cook in the halogen oven at 480°F (250°C) for 3–4 minutes or until the cheese has melted. Serve with grated Parmesan.

pastrami & asparagus pasta

10 oz dried penne pasta

4 oz asparagus

4 oz pastrami, chopped

1½ cups sun-dried tomatoes in oil, drained and halved

1-2 teaspoons lemon juice (to taste)

salt and pepper

To serve

arugula leaves

½ cup Parmesan cheese shavings

Cook the pasta according to the instructions on the package. Drain thoroughly and set aside.

Meanwhile, trim the asparagus, cut the spears into shorter lengths and cook for 1-2 minutes in boiling water. Refresh under cold water and set aside.

Put the pasta in a casserole dish and add the pastrami, tomatoes, and cooked asparagus. Add the lemon juice and season to taste with salt and pepper.

Gently toss everything together and cook on the lower rack of the halogen oven at 400°F (200°C) for 5 minutes to heat through. Serve the pasta in warm bowls with plenty of Parmesan shavings.

Serves **2**   Preparation time **10 minutes**   Cooking time **20 minutes**

chorizo pasta bake

8 oz fresh penne pasta

13¼ oz can chopped tomatoes

4 oz mozzarella, drained and chopped

14 oz chorizo, chopped

½ cup large green olives, pitted

⅔ cup boiling water

salt and pepper

½ cup grated Parmesan cheese, to serve

Put the pasta in a casserole dish and add the tomatoes, mozzarella, chorizo, and olives. Season to taste with salt and pepper. Pour in the boiling water and mix everything together.

Cover with foil and cook on the lower rack of the halogen oven at 400°F (200°C) for 20 minutes or until the pasta is cooked through.

Spoon the pasta onto serving plates and serve with grated Parmesan.

Serves **3**   Preparation time **5 minutes**   Cooking time **18–21 minutes**

baked gnocchi

2 tablespoons olive oil

8 oz mushrooms, halved

1 lb fresh gnocchi

1½ cups ready-made spinach and ricotta pasta sauce

½ cup grated Parmesan cheese, to serve

Heat the oil in a skillet and cook the mushrooms over a medium heat for 3–4 minutes or until golden.

Meanwhile, cook the gnocchi in salted, boiling water for 1–2 minutes. Drain.

Transfer the gnocchi to a casserole dish and gently stir in the mushrooms and pasta sauce.

Place the dish on the lower rack of the halogen oven and cook at 400°F (200°C) for 15 minutes, covering the top with foil if it looks as if it will burn.

Serve this as an appetizer or main course with plenty of grated Parmesan.

Serves **2** Preparation time **10 minutes** Cooking time **16–18 minutes**

french bread pizza

2 small, part-baked
baguettes

1 garlic clove, halved

6 tablespoons tomato paste

¾ cup pureed tomatoes

toppings of your choice,
such as ham, salami, tuna,
olives, sweet peppers, sliced
mushrooms, and mozzarella

salad, to serve (optional)

Put the baguettes on a baking sheet and cook in
the halogen oven at 350°F (180°C) for 10 minutes or
until almost cooked.

Cut each baguette in half lengthwise and rub with the
cut side of the garlic.

Spread each piece of bread with 1 tablespoon tomato
paste, followed by a couple of tablespoons of pureed
tomatoes. Add the topping of your choice.

Put the pizzas on a baking sheet and bake on the lower
rack of the halogen oven at 400°F (200°C) for 6–8
minutes or until the topping is cooked and golden.

Serve with a crisp green salad, if desired, or as an
accompaniment to other pasta dishes.

ham & tomato wraps

2 flour tortilla wraps

2 tablespoons tomato paste

15 cherry tomatoes, halved

6 slices of prosciutto, roughly torn

handful of baby spinach leaves

4 oz buffalo mozzarella cheese, drained and broken into pieces

olive oil, for drizzling

pinch of dried oregano

Put a tortilla wrap on a baking sheet and spread over 1 tablespoon tomato paste. Add half the tomatoes, 3 slices of ham, half the spinach leaves, and half the mozzarella.

Drizzle a little olive oil over the tortilla and sprinkle with dried oregano. Repeat with the remaining ingredients to make a second wrap.

Cook the wraps on the lower rack of the halogen oven at 350°F (180°C) for 10–12 minutes.

Serve as a quick snack or as an appetizer with a small side salad.

Red Pepper Burgers (see page 59)

Cooking pies in a halogen oven

Steak & Kidney Pies (see page 62)

Honey & Sesame Salmon (see page 71)

Serves **4**   Preparation time **10 minutes**   Cooking time **8 minutes**

goat cheese pizza

1 thin and crispy pizza base

2 tablespoons ready-made onion relish

2 tomatoes, thinly sliced

2 oz baby mushrooms, sliced

4 oz goat cheese, thinly sliced

1 tablespoon ready-made green pesto

⅓ cup wild arugula leaves, to garnish

Put the pizza base on a baking sheet. Spread the onion relish over the pizza.

Arrange the tomatoes and mushrooms over the top and add the slices of cheese.

Cook on the lower rack of the halogen oven at 350°F (180°C) for 8 minutes or until golden.

Drizzle some pesto over the top of the pizza and serve garnished with a handful of arugula leaves.

vegetarian dishes

Serves **6** Preparation time **15 minutes** Cooking time **40–45 minutes**

vegetarian moussaka

1 lb potatoes, cut into thick slices

1 eggplant, sliced

1 onion, chopped

2 garlic cloves, crushed

2 red bell peppers, cored, seeded, and sliced

2 tablespoons thyme or marjoram leaves

4 tablespoons olive oil

10 oz cherry tomatoes

1 cup pureed tomatoes

8 oz feta cheese, sliced

1¼ cups plain yogurt

3 eggs

¼ cup grated Parmesan cheese

To serve

Garlic Bread (see page 73)

green salad

Put the potatoes in a large saucepan of boiling water and cook for 5 minutes. Drain and arrange the potato slices on 2 baking sheets with the eggplant, onion, garlic, and red peppers.

Sprinkle over the herbs, drizzle with oil, and roast on the lower rack of the halogen oven at 400°F (200°C) for 20 minutes, turning halfway through the cooking time. Add the tomatoes after 15 minutes' cooking time.

Transfer half the vegetables to a casserole dish and spoon over half the pureed tomatoes and all the feta. Top with the remaining vegetables and pureed tomatoes.

Mix together the yogurt, eggs, and Parmesan and pour over the vegetables. Cover the casserole dish with foil and cook on the lower rack at 400°F (200°C) for 20–25 minutes, removing the foil for the last 5 minutes to brown the top.

Serve the moussaka with chunks of warm garlic bread and a crisp green salad.

haloumi kebabs

1¼ cups basil, plus extra to serve

8 tablespoons olive oil

8 oz haloumi cheese, drained and cubed

1 large red bell pepper, cored, seeded, and chopped

6 button mushrooms, halved

1 zucchini, roughly cubed

13 oz spaghetti

2 tablespoons pine nuts

salt and pepper

Put the basil and oil in a small food processor or blender, season to taste with salt and pepper and process to a puree.

Transfer 2 tablespoons of the puree to a large bowl, add the haloumi, pepper, mushrooms, and zucchini and mix gently together.

Dry-fry the pine nuts in a nonstick skillet over a medium heat for 4–5 minutes, stirring occasionally, until toasted. Set aside.

Thread the haloumi and vegetables alternately onto presoaked wooden skewers. Place them on the upper rack of the halogen oven and cook at 480°F (250°C) for 8-10 minutes or until the vegetables are tender.

Meanwhile, cook the spaghetti according to the instructions on the package.

Drain the spaghetti well and toss with a couple of tablespoons of the remaining basil puree and the toasted pine nuts.

Transfer the spaghetti to 4 warm serving plates and arrange the kebabs on the top.

Serves **2**   Preparation time **15 minutes**   Cooking time **33-40 minutes**

baked butternut squash

1 butternut squash, about 10 inches long

3 tablespoons half-fat sour cream, plus extra to serve

1 teaspoon paprika, plus extra for sprinkling

3 scallions, trimmed and finely chopped

2 tablespoons grated Parmesan cheese

2 tablespoons coarse bread crumbs

Cut the squash in half lengthwise. Use a spoon to scoop out and discard the seeds.

Transfer the squash to a casserole dish, put it on the lower rack of the halogen oven, and cook at 480°F (250°C) for 25-30 minutes or until the flesh is soft.

Put the squash halves on a cutting board until they are cool enough to touch. Scrape the flesh into a bowl, leaving the skins intact.

Roughly mash the flesh with the sour cream, paprika, and scallions.

Transfer the mixture back into the skins and place them in the casserole dish. Sprinkle with the Parmesan and bread crumbs.

Return the squash shells to the lower rack of the halogen oven and cook at 400°F (200°C) for an additional 8-10 minutes or until the tops are brown.

Serve the squash in warm bowls with a sprinkling of paprika and a little sour cream on the side.

Serves 8   Preparation time **15 minutes**   Cooking time **40-47 minutes**

italian bean stew

3 tablespoons olive oil

4 celery sticks, sliced

4 carrots, sliced

3 leeks, sliced

2 garlic cloves, crushed

6 tablespoons white wine

2 x 13 oz cans chopped tomatoes

grated zest and juice of 1 lemon

2½ cups vegetable stock

13¼ oz can cranberry beans, rinsed and drained

13¼ oz can cannellini beans, rinsed and drained

small handful of oregano

Heat the oil in a casserole dish over a medium heat. Add the celery and carrots and cook for 5-6 minutes. Add the leeks and cook for an additional 3-4 minutes.

Stir in the garlic and wine. Bring the mixture to a boil and simmer until the liquid reduces.

Add the tomatoes and lemon zest and juice. Pour in the stock and transfer the casserole to the lower rack of the halogen oven. Cook, stirring occasionally, at 400°F (200°C) for 25-30 minutes or until the vegetables are just tender. The liquid should have reduced and thickened.

Stir in the beans and cook for 5 minutes more. Serve in warm bowls garnished with a little oregano.

Serves 4   Preparation time **15 minutes**   Cooking time **12–15 minutes**

goat cheese tarts

all-purpose flour, for dusting

12 oz prepared puff pastry

5 oz goat cheese, broken into pieces

8 oz cherry tomatoes, halved

1 egg, beaten with a little water

4 slices of prosciutto (optional)

salt and pepper

To serve

arugula leaves

olive oil

large sprigs of basil

Dust your work surface with flour and unroll the pastry. Cut it into 4 pieces, each 3–4 inches square, and place them on a small, nonstick baking sheet.

Arrange the cheese and tomatoes in the center of each of the pastry squares. Season to taste with salt and pepper and brush the edges with the beaten egg.

Place the baking sheet on the lower rack of the halogen oven and cook at 450°F (230°C) for 12–15 minutes or until the pastry has puffed and is golden.

Serve the tarts hot on a bed of arugula leaves, drizzled with some olive oil and garnished with a sprig of basil.

Serves 4   Preparation time **10 minutes**   Cooking time **45 minutes**

italian garlic potatoes

1½ lb baby new potatoes

1 red bell pepper, cored, seeded, and chopped

1 yellow bell pepper, cored, seeded, and chopped

3 garlic cloves, chopped

low-fat oil spray

4 ripe tomatoes, chopped

8 oz mozzarella cheese, drained and diced

½ cup basil leaves, torn

salt and pepper

Put the potatoes and red and yellow peppers in a roasting pan. Add the garlic, season to taste with salt and pepper, and spray with oil.

Place the roasting pan on the lower rack of the halogen oven and cook at 480°F (250°C) for 40 minutes. Stir in the tomatoes and sprinkle with the mozzarella.

Cook for an additional 5 minutes or until the mozzarella is melted. Sprinkle with the torn basil leaves and serve.

Serves 4   Preparation time **15 minutes plus chilling**   Cooking time **5–10 minutes**

spiced veggie burgers

½ cup couscous

2 tablespoons olive oil

1 small onion, finely chopped

2 garlic cloves, finely chopped

1 red chili, seeded and finely chopped

1 teaspoon cumin seeds

½ teaspoon ground coriander

13¼ oz can cannellini beans, rinsed and drained

2 tablespoons roughly chopped cilantro leaves

grated zest of 1 lemon

1 egg, beaten

salt and pepper

To serve

crusty buns

green salad

sweet chili sauce or ketchup

Cook the couscous according to the instructions on the package.

Meanwhile, heat the oil in a skillet and cook the onion, garlic, and chili over a medium heat for 4–5 minutes. Add the cumin seeds and coriander and cook for 1 minute more.

Tip the beans into a large bowl and mash to form a coarse paste. Stir in the onion mixture, couscous, cilantro leaves, lemon zest, and beaten egg. Season to taste with salt and pepper.

Divide the mixture into 4 equal pieces and form each into a patty. Cover with foil and transfer to the refrigerator for a couple of hours.

Put the patties on a baking sheet and cook on the upper rack of the halogen oven at 400°F (200°C) for 5–10 minutes.

Serve the patties between split crusty buns with salad and sweet chili sauce or ketchup.

Serves **4**   Preparation time **10 minutes**   Cooking time **20–25 minutes**

vegetarian chili

2 tablespoons olive oil

1 red bell pepper, cored, seeded, and chopped

1 yellow bell pepper, cored, seeded, and chopped

3 garlic cloves, chopped

2 teaspoons cumin seeds, lightly crushed

10 oz frozen vegetable protein

1½ cups ready-made tomato pasta sauce

⅔ cup water

13¼ oz can kidney beans, rinsed and drained

1 tablespoon Worcestershire sauce

To serve

boiled rice

Garlic Bread (see page 73)

Heat the oil in a skillet and cook the peppers over a medium heat for 5 minutes. Reduce the heat slightly and add the garlic, cumin seeds, and vegetarian protein.

Transfer the mixture to a casserole dish. Mix in the tomato sauce, add the measured water to the jar, swirl it round and pour into the casserole. Stir in the kidney beans and add the Worcestershire sauce.

Cook on the lower rack of the halogen oven at 480°F (250°C) for 10–15 minutes or until the sauce is thick.

Serve with fluffy white rice and garlic bread.

dinner parties

italian halibut & shrimp

4 halibut fillets, each 5-6 oz

2 tablespoons olive oil

4 oz cooked, peeled shrimp (thawed if frozen)

6 small sprigs of lemon thyme

Parmesan sauce

2/3 cup heavy cream

6 tablespoons white wine

3/4 cup grated Parmesan cheese

Arrange the fish fillets on a baking sheet and drizzle over the olive oil.

Set the baking sheet on the upper rack of the halogen oven and cook the fish fillets at 480°F (250°C) for 3 minutes each side.

Add the shrimp and 2 sprigs of lemon thyme and cook for an additional 2 minutes, still at 480°F (250°C). Season to taste with salt and pepper.

Meanwhile, make the sauce. Put the cream in a saucepan and heat gently, beating constantly. Add the wine and Parmesan and continue to cook, stirring, until melted and smooth.

Serve the fish with the shrimp, pour the sauce on top, and garnish with the remaining sprigs of lemon thyme.

Serves 4   Preparation time **20 minutes plus chilling**   Cooking time **about 30 minutes**

beef wellington

2 lb beef tenderloin, trimmed

1 tablespoon chopped thyme leaves

2 tablespoons vegetable oil

2 tablespoons English mustard

8 oz ready-made puff pastry (thawed if frozen)

1 egg, beaten

2 tablespoons butter

salt and pepper

Season the beef with salt and pepper and sprinkle with chopped thyme.

Heat a skillet until it is very hot and add the oil. Cook the beef briefly, turning occasionally, until brown on all sides. Remove the beef from the pan, allow it to cool, and spread mustard over the sides.

Roll out the pastry so that it is big enough to wrap around the beef. Place the beef in the center, roll up the pastry to form a parcel, and brush the edges with beaten egg, pressing them down to seal. Brush the outer surfaces of the pastry with beaten egg and transfer the parcel to the refrigerator for 30 minutes.

Put the pastry parcel on a piece of buttered parchment paper. Transfer to the lower rack of the halogen oven and bake at 320°F (160°C) for 30 minutes until the pastry is golden-brown and the beef is cooked to your desire; test it by inserting a skewer into the beef through the pastry. You may need to cover the pastry with foil for the first 15 minutes of cooking to prevent it from burning.

Remove the beef Wellington from the oven and allow it to rest for 5 minutes. Serve it sliced with vegetables of your choice.

sweet & sour meatballs

1 lb ground pork

1 small onion, finely chopped

1 garlic clove, crushed

low-fat oil spray

1 red bell pepper, cored, seeded, and diced

1 green bell pepper, cored, seeded, and diced

4 oz snow peas

12 oz tomatoes, quartered

4 oz can pineapple chunks in natural juice, drained

6 tablespoons pineapple juice

2 tablespoons soy sauce

2 tablespoons tomato paste

1 tablespoon white wine vinegar

1 teaspoon cornstarch

pasta, to serve

Put the pork in a large bowl and add the onion and garlic. Mix thoroughly to combine and shape into 20 small balls.

Heat a large, nonstick skillet and spray with oil. Quickly stir-fry the meatballs, a few at a time, to brown and seal them.

Transfer the meatballs to a casserole dish. Add the peppers, snow peas, and tomatoes and cook on the lower rack of the halogen oven at 400°F (200°C) for 1-2 minutes.

Stir in the pineapple chunks and pineapple juice, soy sauce, tomato paste, and vinegar and cook, still at 400°F (200°C), for 5-10 minutes or until bubbling. Reduce the heat, cover with foil, and simmer for another 10 minutes.

Mix the cornstarch with a little cold water to make a thin paste. Mix this into the casserole and cook, stirring, until the sauce thickens a little.

Serve the meatballs and the sauce with pasta, such as tagliatelle.

Pastrami & Asparagus Pasta (see page 84)

Summer Fruits Pudding (see page 140)

bacon & bruschetta

5 slices of bacon

1 small onion, chopped

1 garlic clove, crushed

4 cherry tomatoes, chopped

½ baguette, cut into 1 inch slices

5 tablespoons olive oil, plus extra to serve

½ cup grated sharp cheddar cheese

sprigs of parsley, to garnish

To serve

balsamic vinegar

side salad

Put the bacon in a small dish to collect the fat and cook on the lower rack of the halogen oven at 400°F (200°C) for 5 minutes or until crispy. Crumble the bacon slices.

Heat the bacon fat in a nonstick skillet over a medium heat and cook the onion, garlic, and tomatoes until soft. Mix the bacon with the onion and tomatoes.

Brush the bread with oil, place on the upper rack of the halogen oven, and cook at 425–450°F (220-230°C) until toasted. Keep an eye on it so that it doesn't burn.

Place a spoonful of the bacon mixture on top of the toast and sprinkle with grated cheese. Garnish with parsley sprigs.

Return the bruschetta to the halogen oven for a couple of minutes to melt the cheese.

Serve the bruschetta, drizzled with oil and balsamic vinegar, as an appetizer with a small side salad.

Serves **2**   Preparation time **10 minutes plus standing**   Cooking time **40–45 minutes**

garlicky roast beef

2 tablespoons olive oil

3 garlic cloves, crushed

4 cups bread crumbs

1½ cups chopped parsley

½ teaspoon salt

½ teaspoon black pepper

3 lb beef joint

To serve

Roasted Potatoes (see page 124)

seasonal vegetables

Heat the oil in a skillet, add the garlic and cook for 2 minutes, pressing the juice from the garlic into the oil. Add the bread crumbs, parsley, salt, and pepper and mix together.

Pat the meat dry with paper towels. Press the bread crumb mixture onto the joint, coating well.

Put the joint on the lower rack of the halogen oven, cover it with a piece of foil, and cook at 400°F (200°C) for 35–40 minutes, removing the foil for the last 5 minutes to give a crisp crust.

Remove the meat from oven and allow to stand for 15–20 minutes before carving.

Serve with roasted potatoes and seasonal vegetables.

Serves 2   Preparation time **15 minutes plus chilling**   Cooking time **10–15 minutes**

peppercorn steak

2 sirloin steaks, each about 14 oz and 1¾ inches thick

1 tablespoon white peppercorns, crushed

1 tablespoon black peppercorns, crushed

Chunky Fries (see page 123), to serve

Peppercorn sauce

½ tablespoon olive oil

¼ cup unsalted butter

2 shallots, finely diced

2 tablespoons Worcestershire sauce

2 tablespoons brandy

6 tablespoons beef stock

1 teaspoon green peppercorns

1 teaspoon Dijon mustard

3 tablespoons heavy cream

salt

Dry the steaks with paper towels and press the black and white peppercorns into both sides. Cover with foil or plastic wrap and transfer to the refrigerator for 2–3 hours.

Put the steak on the lower rack of the halogen oven and cook at 400°F (200°C) for 5–10 minutes.

Meanwhile, make the sauce. Heat the oil and butter in a skillet and cook the shallots over a medium heat until soft but not brown.

Add the Worcestershire sauce, brandy, and stock to the skillet. Cook rapidly, scraping the bottom of the pan to incorporate the flavors. Add the green peppercorns, mustard, and cream. Season to taste with salt.

Remove the meat from the oven and slice it diagonally. Add the meat to the sauce. Stir to combine the meat juices with the pepper sauce and to warm the meat through. Serve with homemade fries.

Serves **2**   Preparation time **10 minutes**   Cooking time **15–20 minutes**

balsamic-glazed **salmon**

low-fat oil spray

2 garlic cloves, minced

1 tablespoon white wine

1 tablespoon honey

1 tablespoon balsamic vinegar

1 teaspoon Dijon mustard

2 salmon fillets, each about 5 oz

1 teaspoon chopped oregano

salt and pepper

To serve

green salad

new potatoes

Line a small baking sheet with foil and spray with oil.

In a skillet dry-fry the garlic, stirring, over a medium heat until soft. Mix in the wine, honey, balsamic vinegar, and mustard. Season to taste with salt and pepper. Simmer, uncovered, for about 3 minutes or until slightly thickened.

Arrange the salmon on the foil-lined baking sheet. Brush the fish with the balsamic glaze and sprinkle with the oregano.

Put the salmon on the upper rack of the halogen oven and cook at 480°F (250°C) for 10-14 minutes or until the flesh flakes easily with a fork.

Brush the fillets with the remaining glaze and season with salt and pepper. Serve the fillets with a green salad and new potatoes.

Serves 6   Preparation time **15 minutes**   Cooking time **2-3 minutes**

shrimp skewers

3 lemons, cut into wedges

3 limes, cut into wedges

18 large cooked, peeled shrimp

arugula salad, to serve

Sweet chili dip

2 tablespoons honey

1 teaspoon Dijon mustard

1 pinch of crushed red pepper, crushed

Thread the lemon and lime wedges and shrimp alternately onto 6 presoaked wooden skewers.

Make the dip. In a bowl mix together the honey, mustard, and crushed pepper and spoon or brush the mixture over the skewers.

Place the skewers on the upper rack of the halogen oven and cook at 480°F (250°C) for 2-3 minutes on each side until the glaze is sticky and the lemons and limes are beginning to blacken around the edges.

Serve the skewers straight from the oven on a bed of arugula salad.

mozzarella chicken

2 boneless, skinless chicken breasts, each about 4 oz

2 teaspoons pesto

4 oz mozzarella cheese, drained and sliced

Mediterranean Vegetables (see page 128), to serve

Put the chicken breasts in a plastic bag and hit them a few times with a rolling pin to flatten them.

Place the chicken breasts on the lower rack of the halogen oven and cook at 400°F (200°C) for 18 minutes, covering them with foil if necessary so that the tops don't burn.

Remove the chicken from the oven, spread with pesto and add some sliced mozzarella.

Return the chicken to the halogen oven and cook for 3–4 minutes more until the cheese has melted.

Serve immediately with Mediterranean vegetables.

Serves **2**   Preparation time **10 minutes**   Cooking time **12–15 minutes**

herby baked halibut

1½ teaspoons chopped rosemary

pinch of pepper

1 garlic clove, minced

2 tablespoons seasoned bread crumbs

2 halibut steaks, each about 5 oz

1 teaspoon olive oil

salt

To serve

new potatoes

snow peas

In a bowl mix together the rosemary, pepper, garlic, and seasoned bread crumbs. Mash to a paste with a fork or in food processor.

Season both sides of the halibut with salt and put the fish in a lightly oiled baking dish. Brush the fish with oil and press half the bread crumb mixture on top of each steak.

Place the baking dish on the upper rack of the halogen oven and cook at 480°F (250°C) for 12–15 minutes or until fish is flaky.

Serve with new potatoes and snow peas.

side dishes

Serves 4   Preparation time **10 minutes**   Cooking time **40–45 minutes**

dauphinoise potatoes

2 lb potatoes, such as Yukon Gold, thinly sliced

2 tablespoons butter, plus extra for greasing

1 onion, sliced

2 garlic cloves, sliced

1 cup heavy cream

6 tablespoons milk

salt and pepper

Layer the potatoes in a lightly buttered casserole dish. Add the onion and garlic to the dish and season to taste with salt and pepper.

Mix together the cream and milk and pour over the potatoes. Dot with butter.

Cover the dish with foil and cook on the lower rack of the halogen oven at 400°F (200°C) for 40–45 minutes, removing the foil after the first 25 minutes.

Serves 1   Preparation time **5 minutes**   Cooking time **45–50 minutes**

baked potatoes

1 large potato, such as russet

butter

salt

Wash the potato and while it is still damp sprinkle it with salt and prick the skin with a fork.

Put the potato on the lower rack of the halogen oven and cook at 400°F (200°C) for 45–50 minutes.

Cut the potato open and serve with a large knob of butter.

Serves 4   Preparation time **5 minutes**   Cooking time **20-30 minutes**

chunky fries

1¾ lb potatoes, such as
Yukon Gold or russet,
quartered

2 tablespoons sunflower oil

sea salt

Put the potatoes in cold water to soak for 10 minutes.
Drain and pat dry with paper towels.

Place the potatoes in a large bowl. Add the oil and
turn the potatoes to coat thoroughly.

Transfer the potatoes to a shallow roasting pan or
casserole dish and cook on the lower rack of the
halogen oven at 480°F (250°C) for 20-30 minutes until
golden-brown and cooked through. Sprinkle with
sea salt and serve.

Serves 4   Preparation time **5 minutes**   Cooking time **10-15 minutes**

sweet potato wedges

2 sweet potatoes, each cut
into 12 wedges

4 tablespoons olive oil

1 teaspoon crushed red
pepper

sea salt and pepper

Put the potato wedges in a bowl, pour over the oil, and
turn to cover evenly. Add the crushed pepper and stir
to combine. Season to taste with salt and pepper.

Place the potato wedges on the foil-covered lower
rack of the halogen oven and cook at 480°F (250°C) for
10-15 minutes or until the potatoes are tender and
golden-brown. Sprinkle with sea salt to serve.

Serves 4   Preparation time **10 minutes**   Cooking time **50 minutes**

roasted potatoes

2 lb potatoes, halved

6 tablespoons olive oil

salt

Half-fill a large saucepan with cold water. Put the potatoes in the pan, add a pinch of salt, and cover. As soon as the water boils, reduce the heat and cook for 6 minutes.

Drain the potatoes and shake them in a colander to roughen the edges.

Pour the oil into a roasting pan and place in the halogen oven at 480°F (250°C) for 5 minutes.

Put the potatoes into the hot fat and sprinkle with salt. Place on the lower rack of the halogen oven and cook, still at 480°F (250°C), for 25 minutes. Carefully turn them over and cook for another 25 minutes. Check that the potatoes don't burn, covering them with foil if necessary.

Serves **2**   Preparation time **5 minutes**   Cooking time **30 minutes**

parmesan potatoes

6 potatoes, such as Yukon
Gold or russet

olive oil

½ cup grated Parmesan
cheese

sea salt

Scrub but do not peel potatoes. Cut them into 4 large chunks, put them in a bowl, and add oil and salt to taste. Mix together to coat evenly.

Place the potatoes on the lower rack of the halogen oven and cook at 480°F (250°C) for 25 minutes, covering them with foil for the first 10 minutes so they do not burn. Sprinkle with Parmesan cheese and cook for an additional 5 minutes.

Serves **4**   Preparation time **10 minutes**   Cooking time **35–45 minutes**

pilau rice

¼ cup butter

1 onion, chopped

1 cup basmati rice

1 bay leaf

3 cloves

2 inch cinnamon stick

½ cup slivered almonds

2 tablespoons raisins

2½ cups water

Heat the butter in a skillet and cook the onion over a medium heat until soft.

Transfer the onion to a casserole dish and add all the remaining ingredients. Mix well to combine.

Put the casserole in the halogen oven and cook at 480°F (250°C) until boiling. Reduce the temperature to 400°F (200°C), cover the dish with foil, and simmer gently for 20–25 minutes or until all the water has been absorbed.

Drain the rice in a colander if necessary, fluff it up with a fork, and serve immediately.

milk loaf

1½ teaspoon fresh yeast, crumbled

1½ cups whole milk, at room temperature, plus extra for brushing

1 tablespoon corn or maple syrup

2 cups all-purpose white flour, plus extra for dusting

1¾ cups white bread flour

1¼ teaspoon fine sea salt

2 tablespoons unsalted butter, melted and cooled slightly

olive oil, for greasing

Put the yeast, milk, and syrup in a large mixing bowl and beat together. Add the flours and salt and mix with your hands to form a soft, sticky dough.

Pour over the still warm butter and mix this into the dough with your hands. Cover the bowl with plastic wrap or a clean dishtowel and allow to stand in a warm place for about 10 minutes.

Grease your hands and a flat surface with olive oil. Remove the dough from the bowl and knead it for 10 seconds. Form the dough into a round ball.

Wipe the bowl clean, grease it with a little oil, and return the dough ball to the bowl. Leave to rise for another 10 minutes.

Grease a loaf pan and dust it with flour. Divide the dough into 2 equal pieces, shape them into balls, and place them in the loaf pan. Cover with a cloth and allow to rise for about 1½ hours or until almost doubled in height.

Brush the top of the loaf with some milk and cook in the halogen oven at 400°F (200°C) for 15 minutes. Reduce the heat to 350°F (180°C) and bake for another 25-30 minutes or until the top of the loaf is dark brown and the loaf has come away from the sides of the pan. You may need to cover the loaf with foil for the first 15 minutes to make sure it doesn't burn.

cauliflower cheese

1 large cauliflower

2 cups whole milk

1 small onion, finely chopped

2 tablespoons butter

¼ cup all-purpose flour

4 tablespoons heavy cream

3 tablespoons grated sharp cheddar cheese

salt and pepper

Break the cauliflower head into large florets.

Put the milk and onion into a pan and cook, stirring, over a medium heat. Bring to a boil, then set aside.

In another pan melt the butter over a low heat. Stir in the flour and cook for 30 seconds. Gradually add the hot milk and onion and bring to a boil, stirring until thickened. Remove the pan from the heat, stir in the cream, and season to taste with salt and pepper.

Cook the cauliflower in a pan of boiling water for 4 minutes or until tender.

Drain the cauliflower and transfer to a casserole dish. Pour over the sauce, sprinkle with the cheese, then place the dish on the lower rack of the halogen oven and cook at 480°F (250°C) for 5 minutes or until the cauliflower is lightly golden.

Serves **4**   Preparation time **10 minutes plus soaking**   Cooking time **20–25 minutes**

corn on the cob

4 ears of corn

½ cup butter, softened

1 red chili, seeded and finely chopped

handful of chopped cilantro

Soak the corn in a bowl of cold water for 30 minutes.

In a bowl beat together the butter, chili, and cilantro.

Cut 4 squares of foil, each large enough to enclose a corn ear, and place one on each piece. Spoon over the flavored butter and wrap up the corn in the foil.

Cook on the lower rack of the halogen oven at 400°F (200°C) for 20-25 minutes. Unwrap the foil carefully, retaining the butter to serve with the corn.

Serves **2**   Preparation time **10 minutes**   Cooking time **25 minutes**

mediterranean vegetables

2 zucchini, sliced

2 red onions, sliced

1 red bell pepper, cored, seeded, and cut into 1 inch pieces

1 orange bell pepper, cored, seeded, and cut into 1 inch pieces

1 garlic clove, finely chopped

3 tablespoons olive oil

2 teaspoons mixed dried herbs

Put the zucchini and onions in a casserole dish. Add the peppers and garlic.

Pour the oil over the vegetables, sprinkle with the herbs, and toss gently to combine.

Put the casserole dish on the upper rack of the halogen oven and cook at 480°F (250°C) for 25 minutes.

Serves 2   Preparation time **10 minutes**   Cooking time **20-25 minutes**

stuffed peppers

¾ cup couscous

2 red bell peppers

1 red onion, finely chopped

Prepare the couscous according to the instructions on the package.

Meanwhile, cut the tops off the red peppers and core and seed them.

Mix the onion with the couscous. Fill the peppers with couscous and place them on a baking sheet.

Cook the peppers on the lower rack of the halogen oven at 480°F (250°C) for 20-25 minutes.

Serves 6   Preparation time **10 minutes**   Cooking time **45 minutes**

ratatouille

4 tablespoons olive oil

3 garlic cloves, roughly chopped

2 lb tomatoes, roughly chopped

2 red onions, cubed

3 red bell peppers, cored, seeded, and cubed

2 eggplants, cubed

4 zucchini, cubed

salt and pepper

chopped herbs, to serve

Put the oil, garlic, and vegetables in a casserole dish. Mix them together and season to taste with salt and pepper.

Put the casserole in the halogen oven and cook at 400°F (200°C) for 45 minutes or until the vegetables are tender.

To serve, finish with a dash of oil and a sprinkling of herbs of your choice.

desserts

yorkshire cheese tarts

6 oz ready-made shortcrust pastry (thawed if frozen)

vegetable oil, for greasing

½ cup low-fat cottage cheese

finely grated zest of 1 lemon

2 tablespoons golden raisins

2 tablespoons Demerara sugar

pinch of ground nutmeg

1 egg

Roll out the pastry and use a cookie cutter to cut out 12 circles, each about 4 inches across. Put them in a lightly greased 12-cup muffin pan.

Push the cottage cheese through a fine-mesh strainer into a bowl. Add the lemon zest, golden raisins, sugar, nutmeg, and egg and beat together.

Spoon the filling into the pastry shells and bake on the upper rack of the halogen oven at 350°F (180°C) for 10-15 minutes until the filling is just set to the touch.

Remove the tarts from the oven and allow to cool on a metal cake rack before serving.

oaty crumbles

¾ cup all-purpose flour

⅓ cup Demerara sugar

¾ cup rolled oats

½ teaspoon ground nutmeg

⅓ cup margarine

1 tablespoon honey

Line 2 baking sheets with nonstick parchment paper.

In a bowl mix together the flour, sugar, rolled oats, and nutmeg.

Melt the margarine in a small saucepan, stir in the honey, and pour the mixture over the dry ingredients. Mix well and place 16 spoonfuls of the mixture, set well apart, on the prepared baking sheet.

Place the baking sheet on the lower rack of the halogen oven and bake at 350°F (180°C) for 15 minutes or until the cookies have spread out and are golden-brown. Cover them with foil for the first 7-8 minutes of the cooking time so they do not burn.

Remove the cookies from the oven and let cool on a metal cake rack before serving.

vanilla melts

½ cup margarine

½ cup confectioners' sugar

½ vanilla bean

¾ cup self-rising flour

½ cup cornstarch

Line 2 baking sheets with nonstick parchment paper.

Put the margarine in a warm mixing bowl and sift in the confectioners' sugar. Cream together to make a pale, fluffy mixture.

Use a small, sharp knife to slice the vanilla bean in half lengthwise. Scoop out the tiny black seeds and beat them into the creamed mixture. Add the flour and cornstarch and mix to form a stiff dough.

Form the dough into 16 small balls and arrange them well apart on the baking sheets, pressing them down with a fork.

Cover the balls with foil and cook in the halogen oven at 350°F (180°C) for 12-15 minutes until just golden. Remove the foil for the last couple of minutes to brown the tops of the biscuits.

raisin & honey bars

½ cup margarine

½ cup Demerara sugar

3 tablespoons honey

⅓ cup raisins

1 teaspoon ground mixed spice

2 cups rolled oats

Line a 10-12 inch square baking pan with nonstick parchment paper.

Put the margarine, sugar, and honey in a small saucepan and heat gently until dissolved. Stir in the raisins, mixed spice, and rolled oats.

Press the mixture into the prepared pan and level with the back of a metal spoon.

Cover with foil and cook the biscuits on the lower rack of the halogen oven at 350°F (180°C) for 20 minutes. Mark out bars while still warm.

apple & cinnamon ring

low-fat oil spray

1 ¼ cups self-rising flour

1 teaspoon baking powder

½ teaspoon ground cinnamon

12 oz cooking apples, peeled, cored, and coarsely grated

2 tablespoons lemon juice

¼ cup Demerara sugar

⅓ cup golden raisins

3 tablespoons sunflower oil

2 eggs

6 tablespoons skim milk

2 tablespoons reduced-sugar apricot jelly

whipped cream, to serve

Spray a small ring mold with oil.

Sift the flour, baking powder, and cinnamon into a mixing bowl. Mix the grated apple with the lemon juice and stir into the flour with the sugar and golden raisins.

In a bowl beat together the oil, eggs, milk, and jelly. Make a well in the center of the dry ingredients and pour in the milk and egg mixture. Mix together.

Spoon the mixture into the prepared mold and level the surface.

Cover with foil and cook on the lower rack of the halogen oven at 350°F (180°C) for 35-40 minutes. Check that the mixture is cooked through by inserting a skewer into the cake; if it comes out clean the cake is ready.

Allow to cool in the mold for 10 minutes, then loosen the edges with a spatula. Cut into 10 slices and serve warm with whipped cream.

Serves 4-6   Preparation time **15 minutes**   Cooking time **40 minutes**

brownie pudding

½ cup unsalted butter, plus extra for greasing

4 large eggs, at room temperature

1¾ cups sugar

1 cup cocoa powder

½ cup all-purpose flour

1 vanilla bean

whipped cream, to serve

Lightly butter a casserole dish. Melt the remaining butter and set aside.

Beat together the eggs and sugar until thick and pale yellow. In a separate bowl sift together the cocoa powder and flour.

Use a small, sharp knife to slice the vanilla bean in half lengthwise. Scoop out the tiny black seeds and add them to the flour and cocoa powder. Stir to combine. Slowly pour in the cooled butter, mix again, and combine with the egg and sugar mixture.

Pour the mixture into the casserole dish and place it in a larger dish half-filled with hot water.

Cover the dish with foil and cook the pudding on the lower rack of the halogen oven at 350°F (180°C) for 40 minutes, removing the foil for the last 10 minutes to brown the top. The center of cake is supposed to look undercooked and sticky. Serve with whipped cream.

jamaican crumble

2 tablespoons lemon juice

4 teaspoons brown sugar

6 tablespoons water

¾ cup cubed fresh pineapple

8 lychees, pitted and halved

4 dates, pitted and halved

½ banana, sliced

vanilla ice cream, to serve

Crumble

½ cup whole wheat or all-purpose flour

2 tablespoons margarine, chilled

2 tablespoons rolled oats

pinch of ground ginger

2 teaspoons brown sugar

4 teaspoons shredded coconut

Make the crumble. Put the flour in a bowl and add the margarine. Blend with your fingertips until the mixture resembles bread crumbs. Stir in the rolled oats, ginger, sugar, and coconut.

In a small saucepan stir together the lemon juice, sugar, and water over a low heat until the sugar dissolves.

Mix together the prepared fruit in a casserole dish, pour over the syrup, and sprinkle the crumble topping evenly over the fruit.

Cover the casserole dish with foil and bake on the lower rack of the halogen oven at 400°F (200°C) for 20-30 minutes, removing the foil for the last 5 minutes.

Serve hot with vanilla ice cream.

treacle pudding

½ cup butter, plus extra for greasing

6 generous tablespoons corn syrup

½ cup superfine sugar

2 eggs

½ teaspoon vanilla extract

1 cup self-rising flour

custard, to serve

Butter a small baking dish. Put the syrup in the bottom.

Put the butter and sugar in a blender or food processor and mix until pale. Beat in the eggs one by one, then add the vanilla extract. Add the flour and combine until just mixed.

Scrape the mixture into the dish on top of the syrup and cook on the lower rack of the halogen oven at 425°F (220°C) for 20 minutes or until the pudding is risen and golden.

Serve hot with custard.

summer fruits dessert

2 cups summer fruits (thawed if frozen)

3 tablespoons light brown sugar

4 tablespoons blueberry jelly

6 medium ripe pears, peeled, cored, and quartered

1 cup fresh white bread crumbs

2 tablespoons butter, melted

cream, to serve

Put the summer fruits in a large bowl and mix with the sugar and jelly. Add the pears and toss to mix.

Tip the fruit into a deep baking dish. Cover with foil and cook on the lower rack of the halogen oven at 480°F (250°C) for 20 minutes. Insert a skewer to check if the pears are tender; if not, return the dish to the oven for another 5 minutes or until the pears feel soft.

Mix the bread crumbs with the butter and sprinkle over the fruit. Bake uncovered in the oven at 400°F (200°C) for 10 minutes or until the topping is golden and crispy. Serve with cream.

Serves **2**   Preparation time **10 minutes**   Cooking time **15 minutes**

baked bananas

3 bananas, cut into chunks

2 tablespoons butter

¼ cup brown sugar

grated zest and juice of
1 lemon

grated zest and juice of
1 orange

2-3 tablespoons rum
(optional)

vanilla ice cream, to serve

Arrange the banana pieces in a small casserole dish and dot with the butter. Sprinkle with the sugar and lemon and orange zest.

Mix together the fruit juices and rum, if using, and pour over the bananas.

Cover the bananas with foil and cook on the lower rack of the halogen oven at 425°F (220°C) for 15 minutes or until they are piping hot. Serve immediately with vanilla ice cream.

index

acknowledgments

With thanks to JML (www.JMLdirect.com) for lending us their halogen
ovens for the photoshoot.

Executive Editor Eleanor Maxfield
Managing Editor Clare Churly
Creative Director Tracy Killick
Designer Janis Utton
Photographer Ian Garlick
Food Stylist Eliza Baird
Stylist Sarah Waller
Senior Production Controller Amanda Mackie